Taking the Next Step

Taking the Next Step
Teaching Religious Education in Catholic Schools

Richard Rymarz

Brendan Hyde

DAVID BARLOW PUBLISHING
AUSTRALIA

First published in July 2013

David Barlow Publishing
Telephone 02 6533 1810
PO Box 233, Macksville, NSW 2447
www.dbpublishing.net.au
ABN 15 482 647 588

Copyright © 2013, 2020 Richard Rymarz and Brendan Hyde

ISBN 978 1 92133 51 4

All rights reserved. This publication is not to be duplicated or reproduced, either in whole or in part in any form whatsoever without express permission from the Publisher, excepting to photocopy the images within the book for general classroom and project use.

Should evidence to the contrary arise then the Author and Publisher will pursue their acknowledged rights as stated in Copyright Law.

While every effort has been taken to trace, seek permission and acknowledge copyright,
the authors and publishers tend their apologies for any accidental infringement. The authors would be pleased to hear from any copyright owners they may have been unable to contact
and are prepared to negotiate with any rightful owner.

Book design and production by Thymen & Eric at www.exlibris.com.au

Contents

Part 1: Historical and Contemporary Theoretical Perspectives

Chapter 1 : A Brief Overview of Recent Religious Education in Catholic Schools	3
Chapter 2 : Some Contemporary Approaches to Religious Education	14
Chapter 3 : Looking at Religious Education: Perspectives from Key Church Documents	23
Chapter 4 : Contemporary Multiculturalism and Multi-faith Religious Education	32
Chapter 5 : The Human, Cognitive, Faith, Moral and Spiritual Development of Students	42
Chapter 6 : The Perceiving, Thinking, Feeling and Intuiting Elements in the Learning Process	56

Part 2: Pedagogical Considerations

Chapter 7 : The Content of the Religious Education Syllabus	67
Chapter 8 : From Objectives to Outcomes to Lesson Plans	77
Chapter 9 : Planning a Unit of Work in Religious Education	87
Chapter 10 : Differentiating the Curriculum: Catering for Diversity in Religious Education	94
Chapter 11 : Assessment and Evaluation in Religious Education	105
Chapter 12 : Godly Play – An Approach to Religious Education	115
Chapter 13 : Teaching Scripture in the Religious Education Classroom	125
Chapter 14 : Building a Positive Classroom Culture in Religious Education	133
Chapter 15 : Teaching About the Sacraments	145
Chapter 16 : Planning a Eucharistic Liturgy	154
Chapter 17 : Some Challenges in Teaching Religious Education	164
Chapter 18 : The Religious Education Teacher	171

Preface

Teaching religious education to students in Catholic schools in the twenty-first century is an activity that continues to present many challenges. Reflective of the postmodern context in which they find themselves, many students come to Catholic schools from a great diversity of backgrounds. These include both the secular as well as other faith traditions. Those who come from families who indicate that they are Catholic often have little or no connection with their local parish communities.

It is with these, and many other challenges in mind, that *Taking the Next Step: Teaching Religious Education in Catholic Schools* has been written. This book represents a further development of the previous text *Religious Education in Catholic Primary Schools*. In attempting to address some of these challenges *Taking the Next Step* has been designed to assist classroom practitioners in planning and implementing a religious education program that will engage students in learning. It has been written with the aim of providing teachers of religious education with insight into a range of contemporary issues and perspectives which are of relevance to the discipline of religious education.

The text has been divided into two sections. The first section is concerned with an exploration of some of the historical and contemporary theoretical perspectives in religious education. Chapters in this section include an overview of religious education in Catholic schools, the religious and spiritual development of primary school children, and an outline of the perceiving, thinking, feeling and intuiting elements in the learning process. The chapters in this section, while, firmly grounded in the research emanating from the field of religious education and associated disciplines, apply the insights from scholarship to the contemporary context of religious education in Catholic schools.

In the second section of the book consideration is given to the pedagogical and practical aspects of the religious education program. Chapters in this section include differentiating the curriculum, assessment and evaluation in religious education, and teaching Scripture in the religious education classroom. Also, this section gives attention to some of the practicalities of classroom management, as well as to the role of the religious education teacher.

It is our hope that *Taking the Next Step: Teaching Religious Education in Catholic Schools* will act as a guide and resource for your classroom practice.

Richard Rymarz
Brendan Hyde

PART 1
Historical and Contemporary Theoretical Perspectives

CHAPTER 1

A Brief Overview of Recent Religious Education in Catholic Schools

It is the start of the school year in the early 1950s and you are observing the students at a typical Catholic school. The first thing that becomes evident is that there are lots of students – in fact the school is almost *bursting at the seams*. This is a reflection of the high birth rates common at the time – this is the middle of the so-called baby boom. It is not unusual for large numbers of siblings, brothers and sisters, to be at the same school. A closer examination of the student body will also reveal that some of them look and behave a little differently. Their English may not be as well developed as others. These students are new arrivals the country. In the post-war period many places experienced a huge increase in migration. Many of these people came from countries with a strong Catholic heritage such as Italy. There are a lot of teaching religious, especially nuns working at the school.

ACTIVITY 1.1

What were some of the challenges facing Catholic Education in the post war era? What type of religious education do you think was taught in this era?

The post war period was one of great expansion for the Catholic Church in many Western countries. Natural population increases along with extensive immigration meant that the number of students enrolling in Catholic schools increased at a great rate and placed severe demands on the system. Many teachers were members of religious congregations such as the Sisters of Charity of St. Vincent de Paul. In this period it is also worth noting that most students left school in the early years of secondary school to find work. Only a small proportion of students finished high school and an even smaller percentage went on to university.

Religious Education in the Post-War Era

In the post-war era religious education retained the patterns that had been established in the previous decades. This included a dominant role for key resources such as the Catechism. The most important resource was the local catechism such as the *Red Catechism*. This was a small booklet, numbering only 64 pages, consisting mainly of questions and answers, and it set the tone for much of religious education in this era.

Below are three questions and answers from the Red Catechism:

Q. 61 What is the name of the true Church founded by Jesus Christ?

The true Church founded by Jesus Christ is the Holy Catholic Church.

Q. 154 What does Actual Grace do for us?

Actual Grace helps us to know and to do what is right.

Q. 194 How often should we receive Holy Communion?

We should receive Holy Communion frequently, even every day if possible.

ACTIVITY 1.2

> How would you have answered these questions? What does the importance of the Catechism tell you about religious education in this period? What does use of the Catechism tell you about the Church of the time?

Religious Education in the immediate post-war era was more than just learning the Catechism. This is evident if we consider that the Red Catechism contained 236 short questions and answers. Additional materials such as Church history readers and resources produced by religious orders supplemented the Catechism. The important point, however, is that religious education in this period sprang from a very strong **magisterial** sense of Church. This means that it was clear what Catholics believed and how they were to live their lives. These statements of belief and practice could be easily found and an important feature of religious education was to make sure that children in schools could identify and clearly explain these teachings.

There was also a close link between what happened in the classroom and parish and family life. Much of classroom teaching was directed to improving the **devotional** life of students. Implicit here was an assumption that most students lived an active sacramental life as evidenced by regular attendance at Mass and that the family both supported the school and were active members of the faith community.

The Post-Conciliar Era

The most significant event in the history of the Catholic Church in the twentieth century was the Second Vatican Council (1962-1965). The Council signalled significant changes in many aspects of Catholic life. The Eucharistic Liturgy, for example, was reformed – the most notable change was the use of the language of the country rather than Latin. There were many other developments and Catholic education and religious education were directly affected. One of the most obvious changes was the increasing role that lay people played in all aspects of Catholic schools. Whereas leadership and certainly religious education were once the preserve of members of religious congregations, in the post-conciliar period increasing numbers of lay staff were appointed to schools, and soon these people took on significant roles in all aspects of school life.

The 1960s and 1970s were also marked by significant changes in society. One of the biggest, that had a long lasting impact on Catholic schools, was the provision of government funding. Although Catholic schools did not receive the same amount as government schools, the funding removed much of the financial pressure that had been building on parents in the post-war period.

Religious Education in a New Environment

By the early 1960s there was much dissatisfaction with the magisterial and devotional approach to religious education. Many in the field saw the shortcomings of the system largely in the area of its educational deficiencies. In many disciplines, not just religious education, there was a sense that education should involve more than just learning answers to set questions. In religious education an extremely important development was the production of books like My *Way to God* – a series of textbooks designed for use from Prep to Grade 4. These were first used in the early 1960s before the Second Vatican Council but they anticipated many of the developments that the Council would sanction. *My Way to God* marked a new era for religious education and placed great emphasis on the proclamation of the Good News as an integral part of religious education. A key part of this proclamation was the use of scripture.

The extract below is from *My Way to God Book 4*:

> We are on a journey. We are the New People of God, called by our Heavenly Father to make the journey to heaven. Yes, we are all on the Great march to the real Promised Land.
>
> How are we to get there?
>
> Are there any sign-posts? Is there a guide-book to tell us about the place we are going to and what to expect on the way?
>
> Is there Someone who can lead the way?
>
> Yes, our loving Father has given all these helps. The most wonderful of all is the Guide He has given us – His own Divine Son, Jesus Christ. If we follow Him we cannot get lost. We cannot see Him, but He speaks to us through the Church. (pp. 4/5)

ACTIVITY 1.3

> How do you respond to this extract? How would you describe this approach to religious education? If you read this extract to students in class what do you think you would do in the following lesson?

My Way to God is an example of the **kerygmatic** approach to RE. The kerygmatic movement dates back to well before the Council and was associated with some of the leading European scripture scholars. This approach placed great emphasis on the *kerygma* – or the proclamation of the word of God – often best found in scripture, and on students developing a personal relationship with Christ and seeing Christ as the Saviour. The plan of salvation was not something abstract but was meant to be a story that all Christians could appropriate and make their own. The realization by the individual of the personalised message of Christ was to be both liberating and a celebration. Like previous approaches the kerygmatic movement in religious education assumed that students were active members of faith communities. In this schema religious education was seen as being closely identified with catechesis, a term that we will return to later. The goal of catechesis is to make the recipient a better follower of Jesus, and this is clearly seen in kerygmatic approaches to religious education.

Life Experience Approaches

The scene is a Catholic primary school in the 1970s and you are observing an RE lesson. One of the first things you notice is the explosion of colour on the walls. These are filled with posters often displaying a scene from nature along with a short quote from scripture. The classroom has a slide projector which is often used to show audio-visual material. The students are working in small groups discussing their recent holidays and how they managed to act like Jesus in this time. Students sit together at workstations and the teacher, a young woman who has just started to teach RE, walks between them. She encourages the students to express themselves and welcomes all responses.

ACTIVITY 1.4

Contrast the scenario above with that of the 1950s. What are the key differences?

The story above illustrates some of the changes that took place in religious education in the post-conciliar era. One of the main changes was the emphasis given to **life experience.** The Council had renewed interest in the idea that God is revealed in the natural world and in the daily lives of people. Following this much religious education was directed towards getting students to reflect on their own situations and trying to discern God acting in their lives.

An educational resource that illustrates an experiential perspective is *Gathered in Love*. The first edition appeared in 1973 and was produced by the Canadian Conference of Catholic Bishops. Below is an extract from the Grade 3 textbook, topic 1, – "We explore the richness of our world". This illustrates well the emphasis in *Gathered in Love* on placing the students' experiences of the natural world at the centre of the educative process.

If I open my eyes and look I can discover wonderful things all around me
God our Father gave me us the earth to be our home
God said
Let there be earth and water
And there was earth and water
Let there be a sun and water
And a moon for the night
And there was a sun for the sky for daytime and a moon for night
The Holy Spirit helps us to discover
The Father's love for us in the wonderful things he has created

ACTIVITY 1.5

> In an RE lesson of the era what do you think would have followed reading out this extract?

Life experience approaches to religious education created a new language and atmosphere around religious education. They also created some controversy as they represented a significant shift from previous models. The introduction of life experience models also coincided with significant changes in society and in the Church. Religious practices and observance amongst Catholics began to diminish. Life experience models of religious education were well placed to adapt to these changes as they did not depend on an explicit faith commitment on the part of the student. What was critical, however, was that the student was prepared to use their own experiences to try and make religious meaning in their lives. This process is not straightforward, especially as it is to be done on a continual and ongoing basis. The educational basis of life experience models also needed to be refined. The Catholic system expected schools to have some uniformity in their approach, especially in primary levels where students where being prepared, amongst other things, to receive sacraments of Reconciliation, Eucharist and Confirmation. Part of this preparation involved hearing the Church message about what sacraments were and why they made up such an important part of Catholic life. Teachings such as these transcended personal experience although experiences of the sacraments could provide a perfect introduction to the topic.

Shared Christian Praxis

Towards the end of the 1970s a number of educational theorists began to use the insights of critical theory to provide a new curriculum framework for religious education. One of the most important of these perspectives was developed in the United States by Thomas Groome. He coined the term *Shared Christian Praxis* and this model of religious education has been used in a variety of contexts. Whilst valuing the insights of experiential approaches to RE, praxis models sought to place these within a much more rigorous educational paradigm, one which privileged epistemology, that is, the theory of knowledge.

Shared Christian Praxis is derived from Habermas' notion of three types of learning. The first is technical knowledge. In the second the learner makes links between different concepts and how they relate to the wider world. The final stage is emancipatory learning and this allows the learner to become a critical thinker and to weigh up, amongst other things, truth claims.

In Shared Christian Praxis a five-fold pedagogical model is proposed. The first steps are listed below:

1. Naming present action
2. Participants stories and visions
3. Community story and vision
4. Dialogue between stories
5. A decision for future action

For a topic such as baptism the five-fold model could be applied in the following way. As a first step the present action is named with a question such as "what is baptism". Students are then asked to share their stories and understandings of baptism. In the third stage the Church's story about what baptism is and why is it so important is offered. This leads, almost inevitably, to a dialogue between the story of students and the story of the faith community. It is in the final stage, the call to action, that we see the most characteristic feature of Shared Christian Praxis. Here there is some resolve for future action. This is more straightforward in some topics than in others. It is especially suited to units on social justice and the like where there is an explicit action component. In a unit on baptism the call to action could be something like, "how can we make the baptism more central to the life of the faith community?"

ACTIVITY 1.6 – SHARED CHRISTIAN PRAXIS IN ACTION

Shared Christian Praxis as an approach to religious education has obvious significance for adult groups, especially those that have some type of faith connection. How well does it apply to primary or elementary schools?

Try to design a unit based on the five steps outlined above. Pick a topic that you think is well suited to the Shared Praxis approach. Share your ideas on how the unit would develop with others and then critique the unit

What are its strong and weak points?

Guidelines and Religious Education

As the 1970's progressed there was considerable interest in making religious education more educationally relevant. A real problem with a purely life experience approach was that it did not give enough attention to the cognitive aspects of learning. Part of this movement was to use some of the concepts and language used in other disciplines and to apply them to religious education. This movement was supported by Church documents which asked for the same rigour to be applied to RE as was evident in other subjects. To facilitate this development, leaders in religious education in Catholic Education Offices began to develop curriculum **Guidelines**. Guidelines sought to allow teachers working in schools to develop their own curriculum along the parameters set out in the Guidelines. The Guidelines gave religious education a structure and direction but left it up to teachers and schools to shape the curriculum to suit their particular needs. Guideline documents used language that was common in educational circles such as *core objective, learning outcomes and educational goals* and applied these to religious education. The effect of this was to make religious education more educationally focused. Teachers planned lessons to meet specific goals and also developed assessments which were an important part of education in other areas.

Listed below is a key learning from the 1995 *Guidelines for Religious Education for Students in the Archdiocese of Melbourne.*

1.1 Jesus Christ, fully human and fully divine, introduces us into the mystery of God – Father, Son and Spirit. Belief in the Trinity and the Incarnation is central to the Christian faith.

For middle primary the following core objectives relate to Key Learning 1.1:

- recall the gospel stories of Jesus' birth to appreciate his special place in God's plan
- know some of the special names given to Jesus such as Christ, Lord, Son of God
- deepen their understanding of the Pentecost event, and of the presence and action of the Spirit in their lives
- become familiar with some of the symbols and names given to the Holy Spirit

ACTIVITY 1.7

> How would you translate these core objectives into classroom teaching and learning strategies?

Textbooks and Other Educational Approaches to Religious Education

Part of the movement to make religious education more educationally relevant was to develop key resources for students and teachers in the area. A series of textbooks called *To Know, Worship and Love,* for example, were begun in the mid 1990's and can be seen as offering a cognitive framework for the teaching of religious education. They give an overview of important curriculum areas and what level of content is suitable for students of that age. Textbooks also give an indication of key content and what needs to be covered at successive year levels. As with texts in other disciplines, textbooks in religious education seek to meet the educational demands of teachers and students at particular year levels and to aid in the process of curriculum development.

Below is an extract from to *Know Worship and Love* Student Text, Level 3a. Unit 16: Prayer:

> Prayer brings us closer to God. Like growing closer to any friend, this means that we take some time to get to know who God is. When we pray God is with us. Just as you listen to, as well as talk to, your friends, we should listen to God and speak to God…

In the unit there are sections entitled:

- In scripture
- In tradition
- Our prayer
- Aboriginal Our Father
- Did you know?
- Reflecting together at home and at school

ACTIVITY 1.8

What does this extract and section headings tell you about the approach to religious education taken in the textbook?

Textbooks in religious education often establish a basis for future learning by establishing a cognitive framework and identifying key terms and concepts. Below is an extract from the elementary school textbook, *May We Be One*, Year 5:

Unit 1, Theme 3 May They All Be One

St Francis Xavier

Francis was a rich, energetic young man who loved the excitement of social life. He was a brilliant student quite certain of a future career in a distinguished university. For him, all things pointed to a life of total happiness. One day Xavier met Ignatius Loyola a young man studying for the priesthood. The two became close friends. Francis shared his dream of the future. Ignatius listened attentively and then asked a simple question: "Francis, if you live according to your plans, what good will you have done with your life?"

ACTIVITY 1.9

Together with your friends, research other missionary saints. What does this extract tell you about the scope of religious education and expectations placed on students in this textbook?

Some Key Terminology

Three key terms which often arise in the context of Catholic schools are **religious education, catechises and evangelization.** These three terms are often used interchangeably when discussing Catholic schools. It is important, however, to be aware that each term has a distinct meaning.

An educational approach to religious education in the classroom:

Today we are going to look at how Jesus is portrayed in the gospel of Matthew. To do this we will look at the following two stories. As we go through these examples please take down the following words... and add them to your diaries. When we have completed and discussed the stories I will ask you to complete an action box that retells each story and add these to your work diaries.

ACTIVITY 1.10

What is the teacher asking of students in this exercise? What do you think is the focus of the lesson?

Religious education places emphasis on educational goals. Religious education is also vitally interested in teaching and learning processes in the classroom. The goals of the program are often stated in terms of objectives and outcomes and an important role is given to assessment. An educative approach to religious education is centred on the classroom and is expressed in the curriculum of the school. An important distinction that is often made when speaking about religious education is to acknowledge that there is a difference between the general religious education of the school and the religious education that goes on specifically in the classroom. The general aspect of religious education involves the whole school community. It would include a wide range of activities and pursuits, such as attending the founding day at the school, participating in liturgies, listening to guest speakers and taking part in any after-hours events that are designed to foster links between schools and families. The specific sense that religious education is used is to refer to those activities that are associated with the curriculum of the school and what is covered in the classroom.

What is catechises?

Catechesis is a word that is often confused with catechetics. The latter refers to a particular style of teaching that was associated with learning answers from the catechism. Catechesis is a far broader and more inclusive term. One way to describe it is to liken it to all activities that make a person a better follower of Jesus. Notice that this definition assumes that the person is already a disciple or a follower of Christ. This is an important aspect of catechesis. It assumes a faith commitment. It also assumes an invitational and willing demeanour from all those involved. Another way of describing catechesis is to speak of it as a dialogue between believers.

ACTIVITY 1.11

> Describe an activity from the classroom that you would think of as part of the process of catechesis.

SOURCE DOCUMENT

The Religious Dimension of Education in a Catholic School

> There is a close connection, and at the same time a clear distinction, between religious instruction and catechesis, or the handing on of the Gospel message. The close connection makes it possible for a school to remain a school and still integrate culture with the message of Christianity. The distinction comes from the fact that, unlike religious instruction, catechesis presupposes that the hearer is receiving the Christian message as a salvific reality. Moreover, catechesis takes place within a community living out its faith at a level of space and time not available to a school: a whole lifetime. The aim of catechesis, or handing on the Gospel message, is maturity: spiritual, liturgical, sacramental and apostolic; this happens most especially in a local Church community. The aim of the school, however, is knowledge. While it uses the same elements of the Gospel message, it tries to convey a sense of the nature of Christianity, and of how Christians are trying to live their lives. It is evident, of course, that religious instruction cannot help but strengthen the faith of a believing

student, just as catechesis cannot help but increase one's knowledge of the Christian message. The distinction between religious instruction and catechesis does not change the fact that a school can and must play its specific role in the work of catechesis. Since its educational goals are rooted in Christian principles, the school as a whole is inserted into the evangelical function of the Church. It assists in and promotes faith education.

RDECS 68-69

ACTIVITY 1.12

What is the distinction between religious instruction and catechesis? What role can schools play in catechesis? Where does catechesis take place?

Faith and religious education

ACTIVITY 1.13

Today many schools place an important emphasis on religious education as an educative activity that takes place in the classroom. Does this mean that it is opposed to faith development?

How would you answer this question?

Imagine that you are observing a liturgy at the end of a unit on Mary at Grade 3 level. One of the students offers this prayer:

"Mary, Mother of God and Mother of Jesus, we ask you to be with us as we journey through the rest of third year."

ACTIVITY 1.14

Why is this activity part of catechesis?

In the example above, the student is not learning about prayer or describing a particular form of prayer. He is praying. Prayer is always an aspect of catechesis. In this case the student is seeking help from Mary to help him with the trials of the year. This activity assumes faith – a relationship with Christ through his mother Mary. Activities such as these are an intrinsic part of religious education in Catholic primary schools.

Catholic primary schools have a vital role to play in the catechetical process. Faith development is an important aspect of the life of Catholic primary schools. Many of the students are baptized Catholics and their parents enrol them aware of the mission and ethos of the school. Catholic schools also, have the inescapable mark of a faith community about them. The school is often named after a saint: when you walk into classrooms you see religious symbols such as crucifixes and most notable events in the school are usually marked by liturgical celebrations. Many of the topics that are covered as part of the primary school religious education curriculum are pre-eminently catechetical. Take, for example, one of the sacraments of initiation. Students not only learn about, say, the Eucharist, they also receive the Eucharist for the first time. This action is a profound act of catechesis. Teaching children about the Eucharist as a way of helping them prepare for receiving the Eucharist for the first time is an excellent example of the close connection between education and catechesis and how one can serve the other. Many teachers comment that one of the best things they can do to deepen the faith life of their students is to teach them well in religious education. By developing their understanding we can assist students to know and value their relationship with Jesus more.

What about evangelization?

Strictly speaking evangelization is an activity that is directed toward those who have not heard the gospel – that is, those who have not been baptized. If we follow this definition then very little evangelization goes on in Catholic schools as many students are baptized. There is, however, another sense in which evangelisation can be understood. This refers to those who may have been received into the Catholic community some time ago but have never really developed these bonds and are now distant from the faith community. There are many reasons why this alienation has occurred but it is important to recognise that many of the students in Catholic schools fit this description. When dealing with these students the Catholic school can be said to be playing a role in re-evangelisation. This activity is always an invitation. By providing an example of a caring, compassionate faith community the school, through the parents, may encourage families to reengage with the Church and to encounter the gospel of Christ again.

Congregation for Catholic Education. (1997). *The Catholic school on the threshold of the third millennium.* Strathfield, NSW: St. Paul's Publications.

Gathered in love. (1973). Ottawa: Canadian Catholic Conference of Catholic Bishops

John Paul II. (1979). *Catechesi tradendae*. Homebush. St Paul's Publications.

May we be one, Year 5, Born of the Spirit. Ottawa: Canadian Conference of Catholic Bishops.

My Way to God .(1964). Sydney, NSW: E. J. Dwyer

Congregation for Catholic Clergy. (1988). *Religious dimension of education in a Catholic school.* Strathfield, NSW: St. Paul's Publications.

Rymarz, R. (2003). Texts, texts! An overview of some religious education textbooks and other resources used in Catholic schools from the 1950's to the 1970's. *Journal of Religious Education*, 51(1), 50-57.

Rymarz, R. (2011). Catechesis and religious education in Canadian Catholic schools. *Religious Education, 106* (5), 537-549.

Elliot. P. (Gen Ed.). (2002). *To know worship and love* Level 3. Melbourne: James Goold House Publishing.

CHAPTER 2

Some Contemporary Approaches to Religious Education

SOURCE DOCUMENT

General Directory for Catechesis

> It is necessary, therefore, that religious instruction in schools appear as a scholastic discipline with the same systematic demands and the same rigour as other disciplines. It must present the Christian message and the Christian event with the same seriousness and the same depth with which other disciplines present their knowledge. It should not be an accessory alongside of these disciplines…
>
> GDC, 223

QUESTIONS

- In your own words explain what is required of a scholastic discipline?
- How could Religious Education be seen as an accessory?
- How best can Religious Education in Catholic schools be taken seriously?

Activity: Who is Coming to Class today?

You plan to teach a unit on the Trinity to your Grade….class. Like most Catholic schools your class contains students of a variety of backgrounds. There are students with special needs, a couple who are recently arrived migrants and some who have come to the school from other areas. There is also quite a bit of religious diversity. You have students who aren't Catholic. Some who do not have any strong religious background at all. There are a large group of students who are Catholic, in as much as they have been baptized, but have not really engaged with the parish community. There are some who think of themselves as unbaptized Catholics. Finally there are some students who come from families who really try and live out their Catholic faith. Bearing all this in mind:

- What considerations will guide your teaching of the unit on the Trinity?
- Would it make any difference if the class was Grade 1 as opposed to Grade 6?

Educational Goals

The fact that many students in Catholic schools and other Christian schools today do not have a strong connection to an active faith community means that an approach to Religious

Education cannot be entirely centred on catechesis. Another way of looking at Religious Education then places the priority on the educative aspects of the discipline. If we assume that a critical aspect of the school's role is to educate students and to focus on a growth in knowledge then we can follow this logic in Religious Education. In Catholic school classrooms the goal of Religious Education is to help students build up their understanding of the Catholic Tradition in a way that is educationally sound and sophisticated. This goal is not opposed to catechesis; rather it is complementary to it. Religious Education therefore should adopt the same language and rigour of other subject disciplines. Teaching and learning activities that are used in other areas should be directly applicable to Religious Education. Assessment should be used and should have the same scope and depth as in other parts of the school's curriculum.

ACTIVITY 2.1

A strategy for teaching about the Trinity is given below. It is an example of an educational strategy in Religious Education. How would you evaluate this approach?

STEP	DESCRIPTION
Recognition	Make a clear commitment to teach important topics, such as the Trinity, in your class. This does not mean that every lesson should involve complex ideas, but you should realize that these will come up and should be planned for.
Orientation	Examine the existing curriculum to see where the Trinity has been covered in the past. Also recognise that it may be covered again in the future. Topics, such as the Trinity, often require a number of treatments in typical primary or elementary school program. Ask yourself what aspect of the topic will be covered here and what will be done later. Be aware of the age and prior learning of students.
Research	Identify a number of key resources in the area. These can be divided into two types. Firstly, teaching resources used by others to teach the Trinity. Secondly, sources that help teachers understand the Trinity. Be aware that a good deal can be achieved here by some guided selective reading.
Focus	Working with others try to encapsulate as briefly as possible the heart of the issue. What is it that makes the Trinity hard and why do students have trouble understanding it? What is their thinking about the issues involved and, especially, what common misconceptions exist?
Response	Repeat the focus step but now try to encapsulate the Christian teaching on the Trinity that you want to convey to the students.
Educational goals	Using outcome language or similar write down what you expect of students who have completed this unit of work. Some teachers may prefer to do this step after completing the teaching strategies step which follows.

Teaching strategies	This is the critical step. Here a series of teaching and learning activities that will engage students are developed. Rely here on your knowledge as a skilled teacher. Give some thought to how many lessons you are going to devote to the topic. Also plan assessment strategies that will enhance the learning of the students. The outline for the unit begins this process with some suggested teaching and learning experiences and assessment strategies.
Review and consolidation	Try to make some judgement as to the success of your lesson sequence and record what was successful. Also start to develop a pool of resources that have been helpful so that when this topic is tackled again you have a starting point.

Some Approaches to Teaching and Learning: Insights from Vygotsky

And today we start our unit on the Trinity!

Who can tell me something about the Trinity?

Over there we have some books and other resources on the Trinity, working in pairs look through these and answer the questions on this worksheet. Next RE lesson we will compare out answers and put them around the room.

- Comment of the strategies above.
- Do you think they demonstrate good teaching and learning?
- Would you make any modifications?

From a theological angle there are difficulties with an approach to teaching and learning that does not recognize that, in some areas, students will have limited knowledge of the topic being discussed. This is not just because many students today are somewhat distant from an active expression and participation in the Catholic tradition. Some core ideas come to us from the collective wisdom of the Church and these need to be acknowledged not as the end of learning but as the beginning.

"No analysis of contemporary experience can by itself disclose the contents of Christian faith, such as the Trinity, the Incarnation and the Resurrection which are only known for revelation."

Avery Dulles, 'The Challenge of the Catechism', in *Church and Society: The Laurence J. McGinley Lectures, 1988-2007*, (New York: Fordham University Press, 2008), 172.

- Comment on this statement
- What implications do this statement have for the way we teach RE in Catholic schools

This idea of providing students with directed instruction on technical issues as a prelude to a more spontaneous learning dynamic is an idea well captured in some contemporary learning theory, notably in the writings of Vygotsky and his followers. Vygotsky and others have proposed a sociocultural model of learning where teachers and others through participation in activities and reinforcement provide scaffolding for higher learning. As the child gets older the scaffolding becomes more extensive and supportive.

> *Scaffolding Praxis*
>
> Scaffolding of learning can be a difficult idea to grasp in the abstract. A concrete example may help in understanding a basic but fundamental idea.
>
> Imagine that you are taking your class on an excursion to the local cathedral – or significant church. How would you prepare the class for the trip and how would you conduct the tour of the cathedral?
>
> - Write a lesson plan on this topic
> - Where has scaffolding occurred?

Vygotsky made a distinction between what he called spontaneous and scientific concepts in learning. Spontaneous concepts are the result of generalizations based on typical human experience. Many of these are, however, incorrect. A person, for example, may conclude that the sun disappears at sunset and transforms into the moon. No matter how much she thinks about this she is unlikely to change her view without some type of cognitive intervention. Moreover if she does not incorporate this new information any thinking about this topic will be skewed and not reflective of what actually happens when the sun seems to disappear. The way in which the teacher provides this structure need not be direct verbal instruction. It can involve the use of vivid images that take into account the rich imagination of the child. It can involve other types of mediated learning which utilize the talents and potentials of the individual learner.

Vygotsky developed the notion of scientific concepts, which are those that come from the generalized experience of all people, for example, the laws on the movement of planets and be verified in some fashion. In teaching about the solar system, for example, there is much that we know about the basic movement of heavenly bodies. Exposure to the scientific concept allows the student to see the world in a new way or to restructure and raise spontaneous concepts to a new level. Now when discussion arises of how planets and other objects in the solar system move it can proceed on a firm basis. Vygotsky held that student should not be expected to discovery these scientific concepts on their own devices. Rather the role of the teacher was to extend the student by providing enough structure in the form of instruction to allow students to use their new knowledge to reappraise their experience and prior learning.

> "Scientific concepts…just start their development, rather than finish it, at a moment when the child learns the term or word-meaning denoting the new concept".
>
> Vygotsky, L. (1986). *Thought and language.* Cambridge, MA: MIT, p. 159.
>
> - What in your view is the start of learning?
> - Are there any scientific concepts in RE?

If we can see some overlap between scientific concepts and the acquisition of technical theological concepts then we have a proposal that may assist younger Catholics in acquiring the necessary language to be able to, on a firm footing, understand, judge and decide. No one could be expected, for example, to come up with the Trinitarian definition found in the Nicean/Constantinople Creed. It is enormously helpful for topic like the Trinity that young people are given this information as a way of grounding future learning. Whilst the Trinity is not a scientific concept in the strictly Vygotskian sense in that it cannot be verified it does represent a significant example of mediated language learning. A student who is presented with this information in an appropriate manner is much better able to stand outside of her experience and to become an independent thinker rather than one who is entirely dependent on his or her own experience.

ACTIVITY 2.2

How would you do it? List three ways, using different learning styles that important concepts such as the Trinity could be presented

---

The Power of the Image: Using Icons in Teaching

Children have a great capacity to process visual information, so using pictures and images of all sorts has great utility in teaching. Images can also convey a wealth of complex and interesting ideas at once and as a whole. A critical means of communication, especially in the Christian East, are icons. These are highly stylized sacred art which properly understood are not so much pictures but prayers, designed by the artist to open up the Divine. Many of the themes portrayed in icons are the mysteries at the core of the Christian faith. For example there are many famous icons depicting the Trinity. These can be used in RE class as a way of capturing the essence of the Christian understanding of this and many other complex topics.

- Research some icons and build up a collection that could be used in religious education

---

Vygotsky favoured presenting students with precise verbal definitions and students could also receive this type of assistance in understanding complex ideas within the Catholic tradition. A clear, concise and confident presentation of major Catholic ideas should always be mindful of seeing teaching, at its most basic level, as relational. Such a presentation is not, of course, the end of understanding. Rather it empowers the learner to make some type of judgment about what the tradition has to offer and how it sees itself.

> "My teacher of religion in high school was talented; he held a doctorate in theology. But he was absolutely unintelligible when he tried to teach. I learned nothing from him, and still less did he awaken in me a genuine interest in religious matters".
>
> **Romano Guardini (2005).** *Spiritual writings.* **Maryknoll, New York: Orbis Books, p. 69.**
>
> - What implications does this comment have for RE teaching?
> - How can the teacher awaken interest in religious matters?

Implicit here is the idea that the learning potential of the child is far greater than in other developmental approaches. With the correct interplay between the community of learners, students knowledge can be greatly enhanced. The key to utilizing the learning potential of the student is to place them in a strong learning environment which at once challenges them but does not frustrate them. In Vygotskian language this is called the zone of proximal development (ZPD). This can be defined broadly as the distance between the most difficult independent problem solving task a child can do alone and the most difficult problem-solving task a child can do with adult guidance. The adult or older mentor has a critical role to play in learning, they must be able to respond to the needs of the child by on the one hand not excluding them from the learning process by making them passive recipients and on the other from requiring too much of them.

Using Stories in Religious Education

> The power of narrative is "nowhere more evident and justified than in the portrayal of a life".
>
> **Goldberg, M. (1991).** *Theology and narrative.* **Philadelphia: Trinity Press International, p. 62.**
>
> - What is it about stories, especially stories about people's lives that make them so interesting?
> - Can you think of a story about a life that could be used in RE class?

Another useful pedagogical approach to religious education utilizes the power of story. Most people, but perhaps especially children, are captivated by a good story. One way that life stories can change the learning environment is by encouraging learners to be more engaged and less passive. Stories have the capacity to be this for a number of reasons but one critical one is that they can at once get people attention and also convey complex ideas. In this way stories can help to provide scaffolding for future learning.

Stories are effective on a number of levels because human experience is often expressed in story form. We respond to stories because this is how we make sense of the world. One of the key features of life story narratives is that all people are familiar with them in some form and as a result are inherently engaged. This is hard to define in a rigorous way, but a story about a life has the potential to engage the hearer in ways that other types of presentations do not. Narrative can be so compelling because unlike other forms of communication, it is expansive and does not leave too much out. This is not to say that all stories are interesting, but some, and especially those that deal with human life, do have an almost natural appeal. Stories resonate with the reader because in the actions of the protagonists the scope of the human dimension is fully covered.

A Story

Dorothy Day was born in New York City in 1897. Her family were well off and there was lots of time to do fun things. Her father was a sports journalist and it was from him the Dorothy gained both a love of writing and a great interest in investigating how people lived. After leaving university she worked mainly for newspapers and had a real concern for the poor in large American cities. After much searching and becoming a Catholic Dorothy founded, along with Peter Maurin, the Catholic Worker Movement. Dorothy dedicated her life to living as Christ would which she described as turning away completely from sin. She wanted to live totally dedicated to following Jesus. She was also pacifist and opposed war and conflict. She clashed with those in authority. In one exchange she sided with gravediggers who were in dispute with their employer the Archbishop of New York, Cardinal Spellman. She was devoted to helping the poor and disadvantaged in practical ways as well as questioning why poverty existed. Dorothy's commitment to those in need was total. She was deeply moved by Matthew's gospel where Christ is identified with those we serve. Dorothy lived out her beliefs in many ways. She and her daughter lived with the poor so as to try and share their concerns and sufferings. Dorothy died in 1980. In introducing her cause for canonization Cardinal O'Connor of New York described her life a model for all in the third millennium.

We have presented here only the barest bones of the narrative that could be used. The strength of using stories in teaching is that it opens up a whole range of questions. From the story of Dorothy Day there are many themes that can further be explored. Here are some of them:

- Who was Peter Maurin, can we find out more about him?
- Is it possible to live like Jesus?
- What motivated Dorothy to live such a life of radical discipleship?
- What were some of the other causes that Dorothy championed?
- What is sin?
- What is a pacifist? Are all Catholics supposed to be pacifist's
- What is canonization?
- What else can we find out about helping the poor from Matthew and the other gospels?

Narratives also allow for a more purposeful investigation on the part of the students, especially if the topic is challenging and difficult. If their interest has been aroused then activities such as asking student to investigate the concept of heroic virtue has some meaning because they have been presented with an exemplar of such behaviour. More imaginative pedagogy can be used such as asking students to write reflective pieces on what they Dorothy was like as a child. The narrative provides both interest and content in an appealing and unthreatening manner. The quality of the narrative is however, critical. This is where the role of the teacher is vital. It is primarily their job to come up with narratives which at once stimulates student and also open up complex and challenging concepts for them to explore further. What the teacher is doing here is assisting students to think about otherwise difficult topics in ways that allow them to develop their potential. To extend them but not beyond their capacity, especially with material they may be unfamiliar with. This has strong overtones of assisting students to enter the zone of proximal development.

Using Play in Religious Education

Play can be used in a variety of situations in the primary or elementary school religious education classroom. It is particularly appropriate in the early years of schooling and is discussed in further detail in Chapter 12. Play is an important part of how children develop their sense of the world and their place in it. When we come to analyse play we realize what a complex and multifaceted phenomenon it is. When discussing the use of play in educational settings a useful distinction can be made between structured and unstructured dimensions. Unstructured play is spontaneous and allows children to freely expresses interests and use their imaginations in creative ways. The teacher here allows a space for play and may provide some of the props that enrich the experience. Structured play has a stronger framework and can more readily be shaped toward educational goals.

ACTIVITY 2.3

Ready, Set Play!
- When could you use play in Religious Education?
- What could be some of the limitations of play?
- How could a RE teacher use play in units about the sacraments?

The Catholic tradition makes rich use of sacramental symbols to help explain how God acts in the world. The rich symbolism of baptism and the celebration of the Eucharist, for example, involve a series of tangible signs and actions that express the reality of the sacrament. Kneeling during the Eucharistic prayer is a sign of reverence for the action that is taking place, that is, the bread and wine becoming the body and blood of Christ. The pouring of water over the baby's head at Baptism is a symbol of the cleansing action of the Holy Spirit. Children in RE can use play to reenact these actions and to explore, test and analyse their understanding of what the sacraments mean for Catholics.

Play, like all activities, works best if it takes place in a classroom culture that values it and where it is part of an integrated approach to learning. Although play can be spontaneous activity, children will respond best to this activity if they are familiar with it in a classroom setting and know the boundaries that have been set for play. Again like any teaching and learning strategy play in the RE classroom is less effective if it is done too often and without some cognitive scaffolding. If, for example, you were to use play every lesson in scenarios where the children were not aware of the learning framework being followed then the repetition would dull the experience. To take one instance, imagine you were using role play to enact scripture. This assumes that students will have some familiarity with the stories being enacted. This is especially important if the stories have nuance and levels of meaning that may not be apparent after a simple first hearing.

A Type of Play: Using Role Play in the Classroom

A good example of structured play is role play. Here students take on various roles and often reenact or imagine a real life scenario in which they are taking part. It is structured in as much as the teacher provides the context foe the role play. They set out the characters, give background to what is being acted out and assist students to develop their roles. The students can then bring their own experience to the role and expand their cognitive understanding of the topic under investigation.

- Imagine that you are planning a role play based on scripture, for example, the story of the Good Samaritan. Set out the steps you would follow in presenting this to your class.

Arthur, L., Beecher, B., Death, E., Dockett, S., & Farmer, S. (2005). *Programming and planning in the early childhood setting.* Southbank: Thomson Learning.

Chaiklin, S. (2003). The zone of proximal development in Vygotsky's analysis of learning and instruction. In A. Kozulin, B. Gindis, V. Ageyev, & S. Miller (Eds.), *Vygotsky's educational theory in cultural context* (pp. 65-82). Cambridge: Cambridge University Press,

Congregation for the Clergy. (1997). *General Directory for Catechesis.* Strathfield, NSW: St. Paul's Publications.

Karpov, Y. (2003). Vygotsky's doctrine of scientific concepts: Its role for contemporary education. In A. Kozulin, B. Gindis, V. Ageyev, & S. Miller (Eds.), *Vygotsky's educational theory in cultural context* (pp. 39-45). Cambridge: Cambridge University Press.

Marton, F., & Tsui, A. (2004). *Classroom discourse and the space of learning.* Mahwah, NJ: Lawrence Erlbaum Associates.

CHAPTER 3

Looking at Religious Education: Perspectives from Key Church Documents

In discussing religious education in Catholic primary or elementary schools it is important to situate this dialogue within an educational framework. It is also necessary to consider how religious education and schools in general are seen in authoritative Church documents. The importance given to papal and other Roman teachings helps to characterize the Catholic tradition. On important issues such as education the Church can point to a series of statement which give focus and direction to schools and to the place of religious education.

Some Key Church Documents

> The following documents are all easily available on the internet. Select one, open it up and have a look over it. Describe your reaction to the document and list some of the key points you have read.
> - **Gravissimum Educationis**
> - **Religious Dimension of Education in Catholic Schools**
> - **The Catholic School on the Threshold of the Third Millennium**

Gravissimum Educationis (GE)

http://www.vatican.va/archive/hist_councils/ii_vatican_council/documents/vat-ii_decl_19651028_gravissimum-educationis_en.html

The Second Vatican Council (1962-1965) produced one document devoted to education, *Gravissimum Educationis,* and was issued on the 28th of October 1965. GE was one of the last documents promulgated and did not have the impact of some of the earlier conciliar documents such as those dealing with the organisation and daily practice of the Church. It remains, nonetheless, the only document of the council specifically directed to education and, therefore, has particular significance.

Evangelii Nuntiandi (EN)

http://www.vatican.va/holy_father/paul_vi/apost_exhortations/documents/hf_p-vi_exh_19751208_evangelii-nuntiandi_en.html

In December 1975, Pope Paul VI addressed an Apostolic Exhortation to the episcopate, to the clergy and to all the faithful of the entire world. This document, *Evangelii Nuntiandi,* addressed the theme; "Evangelisation in the Modern World". Its focus was, therefore, broad but it had many valuable and important things to say about religious education.

The Catholic School (CS)

http://www.vatican.va/roman_curia/congregations/ccatheduc/documents/rc_con_ccatheduc_doc_19770319_catholic-school_en.html

The Sacred Congregation for Catholic Education is a permanent department of the Vatican. As its name implies, it is concerned with education in the widest sense. *The Catholic School* published by this congregation in 1977 is specifically directed at Catholic educational establishments including schools. CS emphasizes the broad scope of Catholic schools and by implication, religious education within those schools.

Catechesi Tradendae (CT)

http://www.vatican.va/holy_father/john_paul_ii/apost_exhortations/documents/hf_jp-ii_exh_16101979_catechesi-tradendae_en.html

The Apostolic Exhortation of Pope John Paul II, *Catechesi Tradendae*, issued on the 16th of October 1979, is one of the clearest statements ever made by a Pope on the general topic of education. The document was written after the fourth general assembly of the synod of bishops which was held in Rome in October 1977. The theme of the synod was catechesis.

Lay Catholics in Schools: Witnesses to Faith (LCS)

http://www.vatican.va/roman_curia/congregations/ccatheduc/documents/rc_con_ccatheduc_doc_19821015_lay-catholics_en.html

In 1982, the Sacred Congregation for Catholic Education produced another document specifically concerned with Catholic education. *Lay Catholics in Schools* addressed the specific issue of lay Catholics working in schools and can be seen as an important confirmation of the vital and irreplaceable role of the laity within Catholic education.

The Religious Dimension of Education in a Catholic School (RDECS)

http://www.vatican.va/roman_curia/congregations/ccatheduc/documents/rc_con_ccatheduc_doc_19880407_catholic-school_en.html

In 1988 the Congregation for Catholic Education produced a document for "reflection and renewal." The *Religious Dimension of Education in a Catholic School* developed themes contained in earlier documents and focused especially on the religious character of schools.

Chrsitifidelis Laici (CL)

http://www.vatican.va/holy_father/john_paul_ii/apost_exhortations/documents/hf_jp-ii_exh_30121988_christifideles-laici_en.html

The contribution of the laity was further promoted in Pope John Paul II's Apostolic Exhortation of 1988, *Christifideles Laici*. It spelled out the role of the laity as integral to the activity of the Church. The involvement of the laity in "temporal affairs and earthly activities" is seen as essential if the Church is to fulfil its role as a leaven in society.

The Catechism of the Catholic Church (CCC)

http://www.vatican.va/archive/ENG0015/_INDEX.HTM

This document officially released in Australia in June 1995 is described by Pope John Paul II in the Apostolic Constitution, *Fidei Depositium,* which accompanies it, as an authoritative sourcebook for Catholic doctrine. Just as the previous Roman Catechism was developed as a consequence of the Council of Trent, *The Catechism of the Catholic Church* is seen by the Pope as the culmination of the Second Vatican Council and seeks to present the Church's teaching in light of the documents of the Council and subsequent debate.

General Directory for Catechesis (GCD)

http://www.vatican.va/roman_curia/congregations/cclergy/documents/rc_con_ccatheduc_doc_17041998_directory-for-catechesis_en.html

This was released in 1997 by the Congregation for Clergy. It was a development of the 1971 *General Catechetical Directory* which was one of the first official systematic attempts to reformulate the goals and direction of Catholic education after the tumultuous change of the Second Vatican Council.

The Catholic School on the Threshold of the Third Millennium (CSTTM)

http://www.vatican.va/roman_curia/congregations/ccatheduc/documents/rc_con_ccatheduc_doc_27041998_school2000_en.html

This document was released at the end of 1997 by the Congregation for Catholic Education. It sort, amongst other things, to set out a vision for Catholic schools in a variety of educational and cultural contexts.

ACTIVITY 3.1

Provide a summary of one of the documents mentioned above. In your summary include:

- How the document is structured
- How it is addressed to
- Key points
- How it concludes
- Your reaction to the document

Some Key Themes

1. Schools and the Formation of the Person and of Culture

One of the key themes that emerge from a number of Church documents related to education is the importance of the school in human formation. GE clearly sees religious education as more than the mere imparting of information. Indeed religious education needs to be seen in the context of education of the whole person. This distances the concept of religious education from didactic or formal instruction. Authentic religious education is more than learning rote formulas and definitions, which were techniques of historical significance. Central to this notion of educating the whole person, and one of the dominant themes of GE, is the role of the school in facilitating the transmission of culture to students. Here culture is understood as the broad sum of beliefs, values, tradition and history that underpin every society. Culture can be understood in this way in a general sense. It also has a specific meaning when it is referred to as culture of the Church or Christian culture. Education involves the students being imbued with the knowledge and appreciation of the culture of society and the specific culture of the Church.

> ...among the various organs of education the school is of outstanding importance. In nurturing the intellectual faculties which is its special mission, it develops a capacity for sound judgments and introduces the pupils to the cultural heritage bequeathed to them by former generations. It fosters a sense of values and prepares them for professional life. By providing for friendly contacts between pupils of different characters and backgrounds it encourages mutual understanding ...
>
> GE 5

Education is described as an "inalienable right" (GE 1) and part of the general formation of all. Religious education is seen as part of the culture and heritage that effective education must transmit. How this is transmitted is not prescribed and GE places great reliance on contemporary practice.

> ... Due weight being given to the advances in psychological, pedagogical and intellectual sciences, children and young people should be helped to develop harmoniously their physical, moral and intellectual qualities ...
>
> GE 1

CS also emphasizes the broad scope of Catholic schools and by implication, religious education within those schools. The schools aims are summarized as,

> ... it (the school) must develop persons who are responsible and inner directed, capable of choosing freely in conformity with their conscience.
>
> CS 31

Within this general framework the religious education curriculum takes on special significance as it is committed to the critical transmission of culture, a point central to many of the documents quoted here and which lies at the core of Catholic education. LCS develops the broad conception of education mentioned in *Gravissimum Educationis*. This notion involves the integral formation of the whole person. The function of the school is the development of individuals and to allow individuals to understand and to be active and informed participants in the culture to which they belong. Formal religious education or instruction is one aspect of this integral formation. Catholic educators, therefore, seek to introduce pupils in their care to the values inherent in Catholic culture, chief amongst these being a Christian conception of the human person.

> ... the school must be concerned with constant and careful attention to cultivating in students the intellectual, creative, and aesthetic faculties of the human person ... to introduce them to the cultural patrimony handed down from previous generations ...
>
> LCS 12

2. Religious Education is Important and Needs to be Taught Well

Another key theme in Church documents is the importance of RE in Catholic schools. Religious education needs to be sensitive to the culture and needs of the audience but the approach adopted should be planned and systematic.

> ... young people need to learn through systematic religious teachings the fundamental teachings ... which God has wished to convey to us ... the methods used must be adapted to the age, culture and aptitude of the persons concerned ...
>
> EN 44

ACTIVITY 3.2

> Good morning class! We should have RE now but we just need to......
>
> - What are some of the pressures on given RE an explicit place in the school curriculum?

Education in the faith needs to be explicit and systematic. This means that religious education should have a defined and valued place in the curriculum and not be replaced by other activities as the need arises.

> ... it must be emphasized that, while such teaching is not merely confined to 'religious classes' ... it must, nevertheless, also be imparted explicitly and in a systematic manner ... the fundamental difference between religious and other forms of education is that its aim is not simply intellectual assent to truths but also a total commitment of one's whole being to the person of Christ ...
>
> CS 50

Pope John Paul II elaborates further on the framework for religious education in Catholic schools:

> In view of practical difficulties, attention must be drawn to some of the characteristics of this instruction:
>
> It must be systematic, not improvised but programmed to reach a precise goal;
>
> It must deal with essentials, without any claim to tackle all disputed questions or to transform itself into theological research or scientific exegesis;
>
> It must nevertheless be sufficiently complete, not stopping short at the initial proclamation of the Christian mystery such as we have in the *kerygma*;

> It must be an integral Christian initiation, open to all other factors of Christian life.
>
> CT 21

One useful way of conceptualizing the style and authority of religious education in schools is to compare it to other disciplines. A number of Church documents make the point that there should be substantial overlap between religious education and other subjects in terms of cognitive level of content, teaching demands and assessment.

> It is necessary, therefore, that religious instruction in schools appear as a scholastic discipline with the same systematic demands and the same rigour as other disciplines. It must present the Christian message and the Christian event with the same seriousness and the same depth with which other disciplines present their knowledge. It should not be an accessory alongside of these disciplines, but rather it should engage in a necessary inter-disciplinary dialogue.
>
> GDC 73

A critical focus of the Catholic school is on the education of the whole person. Due to a variety of factors the enrolment patterns in Catholic schools all over the Western world have changed in recent decades. There are now large numbers of non-Catholic students attending Catholic schools in countries where the schools developed to provide an education for an overwhelming Catholic clientele. In addition, there are large numbers of students and parents associated with Catholic schools who while Catholic in a canonical sense, that is, they have been baptized, are not active members of the faith community.

In these circumstances the catechetical goals of Catholic schools need to be reformulated. Catechesis depends on an active faith response. The Catechism of the Catholic Church sees catechesis as an integral part of the Church's mission. It is, however, a diverse and broad concept but is associated at a fundamental level with education.

> … catechesis is an education in the faith of children, young people, and adults … in an organic and systematic way, with a view to initiating the hearers into the fullness of Christian Life …
>
> CCC 5

This does not imply that those to be catechized have a particularly strong or well developed faith but rather that there is some initial faith response that exists within the context of an active worshipping community. In Catholic schools today, however, there are increasing numbers of students who are not members of faith communities and therefore the religious education program needs to be broader than a strictly catechetical program.

> There is a close connection, and at the same time a clear distinction, between religious instruction and catechesis, or the handing on of the Gospel message … The distinction comes from the fact that, unlike religious instruction, catechesis presupposes that the hearer is receiving the Christian message as a salvific reality. Moreover, catechesis takes place within a community living out its faith at a level of space and time not available to a school: a whole lifetime.
>
> RDECS 68

3. Importance of the Teacher

The extract below is from Christifideles Laici:

> THE LAY MEMBERS of Christ's Faithful People (Christifideles Laici), whose "Vocation and Mission in the Church and in the World Twenty Years after the Second Vatican Council" was the topic of the 1987 Synod of Bishops, are those who form that part of the People of God which might be likened to the labourers in the vineyard mentioned in Matthew's Gospel: "For the Kingdom of heaven is like a householder who went out early in the morning to hire labourers for his vineyard. After agreeing with the labourers for a denarius a day, he sent them into his vineyard" (Mt 20:1-2).
>
> The gospel parable sets before our eyes the Lord's vast vineyard and the multitude of persons, both women and men, who are called and sent forth by him to labour in it. The vineyard is the whole world (cf. Mt 13:38), which is to be transformed according to the plan of God in view of the final coming of the Kingdom of God.

CL 1

- What scriptural analogies are used to describe the role of the laity?
- How well do you think this extract contextualizes the work of RE teachers in Catholic schools?
- What demands does it place on RE teachers and are these demands realistic?

RE teachers are required to display integrity in keeping with the subject matter they are presenting. This ties in with the goal of religious education being concerned with more than just passing on information. This process is dependent on RE teachers witnessing to what they teach.

> …they (teachers) should therefore be prepared for their work with special care, having the appropriate qualifications and adequate learning both religious and secular. They should also be skilled in the art of education in accordance with the discoveries of modem times. Possessed by charity both towards their pupils, and inspired by an apostolic spirit, they should bear testimony by their lives and their teaching to the Teacher, who is Christ…

GE 8

Pope Paul VI stressed the role of the laity in the specific task of imparting religious instruction or catechesis. The Pope here is recognizing the important contribution that members of the Church, who are not consecrated ministers or members of religious communities, play in the evangelizing mission of the Church.

> … it is necessary above all to prepare good instructors…teachers who are desirous of perfecting themselves in this superior art…

EN 44

Pope Paul also stresses the unique responsibility of those involved in the work of evangelization. Chief amongst these is the need to be an effective witness and to display those qualities that reflect a deep and abiding commitment to Christ.

> ... modern man listens more willingly to witnesses than to teachers and if it does listen to teachers, it is because they are witnesses ...
>
> EN 41

This notion of the teacher as witness is repeated in many documents and stresses that teachers need to be animate, in an authentic way, the beliefs and values that they teach about. This recognizes that in order to be able to lead another on the path of knowing Christ better more than content knowledge is required.

> ... Whoever is called to teach Christ must first seek the surpassing worth of knowing Christ Jesus ...
>
> CCC 428

REACTION QUESTION

Can the RE teacher be effective without being a witness?

The Catholic School and the Society: Challenge and Response

Read the quote below from the introduction of *The Catholic School on the Threshold of the Third Millennium*:

> On the threshold of the third millennium education faces new challenges which are the result of a new socio-political and cultural context. First and foremost, we have a crisis of values which, in highly developed societies in particular, assumes the form, often exalted by the media, of subjectivism, moral relativism and nihilism. The extreme pluralism pervading contemporary society leads to behaviour patterns which are at times so opposed to one another as to undermine any idea of community identity. Rapid structural changes, profound technical innovations and the globalization of the economy affect human life more and more throughout the world. Rather than prospects of development for all, we witness the widening of the gap between rich and poor, as well as massive migration from underdeveloped to highly-developed countries. The phenomena of multiculturalism and an increasingly multi-ethnic and multi-religious society is at the same time enrichment and a source of further problems. To this we must add, in countries of long-standing evangelization, a growing marginalization of the Christian faith as a reference point and a source of light for an effective and convincing interpretation of existence.
>
> CSTTM 1

- Do you agree with this analysis?

- What challenges does this assessment of society place before Catholic schools?
- If you were writing an opening paragraph on *Catholic Schools in the Second Decade of the Third Millennium and Beyond* what key issues would you raise?

Buchanan, M.T., & Hyde, B. (2006). The role of the religion teacher: Ecclesial and pedagogical perceptions. *Journal of Christian Education, 49* (2), 23-34.

Ryan, M. (2006). *Religious education for students in Catholic schools: An introduction for Australian students.* Melbourne: David Lovell.

Church Document Websites

Catechesi Tradendae

http://www.vatican.va/holy_father/john_paul_ii/apost_exhortations/documents/hf_jp-ii_exh_16101979_catechesi-tradendae_en.html

Chrsitifidelis Laici

http://www.vatican.va/holy_father/john_paul_ii/apost_exhortations/documents/hf_jp-ii_exh_30121988_christifideles-laici_en.html

Evangelii Nuntiandi

http://www.vatican.va/holy_father/paul_vi/apost_exhortations/documents/hf_p-vi_exh_19751208_evangelii-nuntiandi_en.html

General Directory for Catechesis

http://www.vatican.va/roman_curia/congregations/cclergy/documents/rc_con_ccatheduc_doc_17041998_directory-for-catechesis_en.html

Gravissimum Educationis

http://www.vatican.va/archive/hist_councils/ii_vatican_council/documents/vat-ii_decl_19651028_gravissimum-educationis_en.html

Lay Catholics in Schools: Witnesses to Faith

http://www.vatican.va/roman_curia/congregations/ccatheduc/documents/rc_con_ccatheduc_doc_19821015_lay-catholics_en.html

The Catechism of the Catholic Church

http://www.vatican.va/archive/ENG0015/_INDEX.HTM

The Catholic School

http://www.vatican.va/roman_curia/congregations/ccatheduc/documents/rc_con_ccatheduc_doc_19770319_catholic-school_en.html

The Catholic School on the Threshold of the Third Millennium

http://www.vatican.va/roman_curia/congregations/ccatheduc/documents/rc_con_ccatheduc_doc_27041998_school2000_en.html

The Religious Dimension of Education in a Catholic School

http://www.vatican.va/roman_curia/congregations/ccatheduc/documents/rc_con_ccatheduc_doc_19880407_catholic-school_en.html

CHAPTER 4

Contemporary Multiculturalism and Multi-faith Religious Education

The multicultural composition of Catholic schools, particularly those in large cities in western countries, is a relatively recent phenomenon. In many western countries, the period immediately following the Second World War was one which saw extensive immigration. This, along with natural population increases, meant that the numbers of students enrolling in Catholic schools increased at a great rate and placed severe demands on the system (Healy, Hyde & Rymarz, 2004). During this period, Catholic schools usually received little or no government funding and as a result, they were not as well equipped as corresponding government schools.

Today, Catholic schools in most large cosmopolitan cities in western countries host students from a wide variety of cultural backgrounds. In many cases, these students come to Catholic schools from cultural backgrounds in which Christianity (in particular Catholicism) is not the dominant faith tradition. In some instances, Catholic schools also host students from countries such as Lebanon, Iraq and Egypt who are Catholic, but not *Roman* Catholic. These students belong to what have become known as the *Eastern Rite* traditions of Catholicism. For example, Catholic students from Lebanon often belong to the *Maronite* tradition. Catholic students from Iraq often belong to the *Chaldean* rite. Students from these traditions may celebrate the Sacraments at different times in their lives to most Roman Catholics, and in some cases, their celebration of particular feasts and liturgical seasons, such as Christmas, also occur at slightly different times.

As well, contemporary Catholic schools host students from a range of religious traditions other than Christianity. It is not uncommon for Catholic schools in large cities to host students from Islamic, Buddhist and Hindu backgrounds, to name just a few. Such a multi-faith composition in Catholic schools requires sensitivity, careful curriculum planning, and ideally, an attention to multi-faith religious educational perspectives.

Catering for such diversity in the religious education classroom can then prove challenging for even the most experienced of religious educators. This chapter explores broadly the issue of multiculturalism in religious education and multi-faith religious education. It highlights some of the implications these have for religious education generally.

Two Approaches to Multiculturalism

In terms of multiculturalism and religious education, there are two common, but inadequate approaches that have been held by teachers in relation to the religious education curriculum. These comprise the "assimilationist approach" and the "ethnic additive" model (Goosen, 1985). They are best described through practical example via the case study which is presented below for each approach.

The Assimilationist Approach

Case Study 1: They should do as we do.

> Missal and Wadi are two students whose families come from Lebanon. They are members of the *Maronite* rite of the Catholic Church. They are both in the same Year 4 class of the local Catholic primary/elementary school, which is preparing to celebrate Confirmation. Both Missal and Wadi celebrated Confirmation as infants when they were baptized. However, Michelle, the Year 4 classroom teacher is not familiar with this practice. How can they both have already "made their Confirmation", she thinks. Catholic children don't do this until they reach the age of at least 6 or 7, and in this parish, they "make this Sacrament" when they are in Year 4. Michelle decides to speak to the Religious Education Coordinator (REC) about this matter. "Yes, that's correct", sighs the REC, "because they come from the Maronite tradition, both Missal and Wadi will have already celebrated this Sacrament. I know, it's a real nuisance, isn't it! It complicates our planning."
>
> "Yes, it does," agrees Michelle. "How can this be a special time for them when they are clearly out of step with the Roman Catholic tradition? And given that they were both born in Australia, why can't they just be like the rest of us?"

ACTIVITY 4.1

> Spend a moment reflecting Case Study 1. What is your reaction to this situation? Share your response with a partner.

Case Study 1 above is an example of two teachers who have adopted an assimilationist philosophy. The assimilationist approach can be characterized by the disapproval of any gathering of migrants into ethnic groups. Broadly, assimilationists insist that those from other cultural backgrounds should mix with everything "Australian" or "Canadian" or "English", depending upon the country in which those from other cultural backgrounds are now living. They argue that since migrants have chosen to come to a particular country to live, they should learn the language of that country and do things the way they are done in that country (Goosen, 1985). Such an attitude is in keeping with the assimilationist philosophy. In sociological terms, it accepts that minority groups can be received into any particular society, but that those groups are expected to assimilate into the culture of the dominant group, suppressing the many elements their own culture, including the language, or "mother-tongue" of their culture. Goosen notes that language is a powerful cultural vehicle. It can be used to either promote a culture, or indeed to suppress a minority cultural group by, for example, insisting at everyone speak the language of the dominant group, ignoring or pretending not to understand those who speak in their own cultural language.

In terms of religious education, the assimilationist approach could mean that minority groups in Catholicism, such as those from the Eastern Rite traditions, be expected to change their religious practices so as to conform to the Anglo-Irish expression of Catholic

Christianity. This could include the ways in which the religious tradition is passed on from parent to child, in favor of the way in which it is taught in the context of the religious education classroom.

The "Ethnic Additive" Approach

Case Study 2: An "Italian" saints' day.

> Daniel is a Year 6 teacher at Our Lady's Catholic primary/elementary school. Most of the students who attend Our Lady's school come from an Anglo-Saxon background. However, over the course of the last five years, a number of children from Italian families have moved into the local area, and now attend the school. The feast of All Saints is approaching, and the Year 6 planning team have met together to plan a religious education unit with a focus on saints. "I have an idea," says David during the planning meeting. "Why don't we plan an *Italian saints'* day as a part of this unit? We could plan a series of activities that explore the lives of typical Italian saints…There is St. Anthony for starters…and many of the other children who are not Italian could learn a lot from this day…"

ACTIVITY 4.2

> Spend a moment reflecting Case Study 2. What is your reaction to this situation? Does this seem like a reasonable thing to do? Share your response with a partner.

In this particular approach, proponents recognize that some concessions need to be made in situations in which minority ethnics groups are represented. For instance, and in a religious educational context, schools in which Italian students are present may include in the RE curriculum a discussion of popular Italian saints within an appropriate unit of work, as was planned in Case Study 2 above. Similarly, if there are a number of Chaldean Catholic students present in the classroom, reference might occasionally be made to the way in which the Eucharist, or other Sacraments are celebrated within that particular rite.

On the face of it, this may seem like a reasonable approach. However, it really is a minimalist approach, and one that is tokenistic. It doesn't necessarily value the culture of the ethnic minority group, and doesn't embed within the curriculum the many elements of various cultural groups which could be explored. Further, Goosen (1985) argues that in applying this particular model, the implication is that nothing at all is done if a particular school has no ethnic groups represented in its student population. Goosen argues that it can become difficult for teachers to see why any changes might need to be made in a curriculum if the school or class population is entirely Anglo-Celtic. And the crucial point which is overlooked is that students will eventually move out of the sheltered and mono-cultural environment of the school into a society which continues to become increasingly multicultural and multi-faith in its composition.

Some writers have suggested various means by which the religious education curriculum might avoid both of these inadequate approaches in adapting its approach to RE in the light of multiculturalism. For example, Foster (1991) outlines four implications for a multicultural religious education. These are outlined in Table 4.1 below.

Table 4.1. Implications for a multicultural religious education.

Teaching for cultural awareness
A focus on helping students begin to discover the wonder to be found in the particularity of human experience.
Teaching for cultural affirmation
Multicultural religious education makes possible the self-affirmation by students of their own cultural heritage as a significant resource for hearing and responding to the Gospel. Cultural resources include art, music, literature, architecture, and the like.
Teaching for cultural appreciation and respect
Multicultural religious education creates opportunities to discover resources for listening to and responding to the Gospel in other cultures. It involves a dialogical conversation across cultural differences in the recognition of otherness.
Teaching for participation in other cultures
An emphasis on the creation of hospitable places for sharing, testing and practicing the ways of knowing, relating, responding, serving and celebrating integral to specific cultural patterns of being faithful.

Foster, 1991

ACTIVITY 4.3

With a partner, discuss your response to the implications as presented in the above table.

In a similar vein, Goosen (1985) outlined 7 implications of multiculturalism for religious education. These implications include a clear focus on both different cultural ways of being Catholic, *and* multi-faith cultures. They are presented in Table 4. 2 on the next page.

Table 4.2: Goosen's implications for multicultural religious education

Identify the world religions
Being aware of Christianity, Judaism, Islam, Buddhism and Hinduism, and include opportunities for the study of these traditions within the religious education curriculum.
Identify various Christian denominations
There is a focus here on ecumenism and the different ways of practicing Christianity, as well as a study of the Orthodox Church.
Identify various rites within the Catholic Church
Raise the awareness of the existence of other Catholic rites – Armenian, Byzantine, Coptic, Greek, Maronite, Melchite, Ukranian, and Chaldean. This presents the Catholic Church as being anything but monolithic.
Relativize, whilst appreciating one's own religion
Move from the absolutist position to seeing all cultures including one's own as different, but as having their own validity. This does not mean that one's own customs are devalued, but recognizes the authenticity in various traditions including one's own.
Examine culture and the origins of religious beliefs and practices
Implied in the goal above, but stressing that the concept of culture needs to be thoroughly analyzed.
Examine and understand the phenomenon of religious acculturation
This is the process whereby a person from one religious tradition acquires some of the practices and customs of another.
Recognize the fact of the changed composition of many western Christian Churches
In many western countries, the Catholic Church has become less and less dominated by any one particular culture to being truly multicultural.

Adapted Goosen (1985)

The implications as outlined by Goosen (1985) above begin to steer us in the direction of the issue of multi-faith aspects in religious education. This is a pertinent issue. Although some secondary/high schools' Catholic religious education curricula address this aspect, generally speaking, most approved diocesan religious education syllabi and curricula, particularly at the primary/elementary school level, often neglect the multi-faith aspect of religious education. In an environment in which, for many reasons, students from a range of faith backgrounds other than Christianity find themselves in Catholic schools, the multi-faith aspect of religious education can no longer be ignored.

Multi-faith Religious Education

Goldburg (2007a) notes that in order to be educated well in terms of contemporary religion, students need to know something of other religious traditions while simultaneously developing a deeper understanding of their *home* tradition. As such, Goldburg (2007a,

2007b) advocates the *study of religion*, in which the major world religions feature within the classroom religious education program, as being a way forward. Two possible approaches which may achieve this aim are briefly outlined below. While the first – the social constructivist approach – has been developed for use with secondary/high school students in mind, the possibility for adaptation to the primary/elementary school context is a real possibility. The second – the dialogical approach to religious education – was developed by Julia Ipgrave at the University of Warwick in England specifically for use in the primary/elementary school context.

Social Constructivist Approaches

Social constructivist approaches represent one possibility here. This approach recognizes that human beings construct knowledge within an environment and in the process, both people and the environment are changed. It recognizes the learning acquired by the individual from her or his own culture, such as language, ways of thinking, and symbol systems, all of which dictate how and what is actually learnt. It also takes account of the learner's social interaction with knowledgeable members of society, without whom it is impossible to acquire social meanings or symbol systems and how use them. Social constructivist approaches encourage the learner to be actively involved in the learning process because each learner constructs her or his own understanding – they do not simply mirror and reflect what they have read or been told.

British religious educator Michael Grimmitt (2000) provided one model for how social constructivism might operate in a religious education classroom. He labels three steps in this process:

1. *Preparatory Pedagogical Constructivism (PPC)*. This engages students in an enquiry into their own experience in order to prepare them for an encounter with an item of religious content. The teacher assists the students' enquiries by asking questions and making interventions which may include practical, group-focused activities. For example, a teacher might ask: Why do people pray? Where do people pray? Does it always have to be in a building? What religious dress or religious objects do people use for prayer? (cf. Goldburg, 2007b).

2. *Direct Pedagogical Constructivism (DPC)*. Here, students are given an item of religious content without explanation so that it becomes the stimulus for them to begin to construct their own meaning and understanding it, while at the same time drawing on their own experiences and the experiences of the group. For example, students might be provided with some religious artifacts from Judaism as the items of religious content. They are shown these without any explanation, and their task is to try to construct their own meaning. Students may be presented with a prayer shawl and scroll, and given questions such as: Describe the prayer shawl – what are its features? Describe the scroll – what might it be used for? (cf. Goldburg, 2007b).

3. *Supplementary Pedagogical Constructivism (SPC)*. In this stage students are provided with additional information about the religious content which enables their construction and interpretations to deepen and, ideally, to consider alternative

perspectives. The previous interpretations of the students should not be abandoned in the face of this new knowledge. Rather the intention is that they engage in an interpretive process in which the new knowledge is critiqued and either accommodated within their own understanding or questioned further. For example, the teacher might provide students with some quotes from people talking about how they feel when they wear the prayer shawl and how it helps to focus them on prayer. The teacher might tell the students that nearly all Jewish prayers are in Hebrew, and ask students to discuss why this might be so.

In using this approach contestable material, primary and secondary sources which offer differing views on the topic under consideration need to be included in addition to primary texts and workbooks. The learning should be interactive and should build upon what the students already know. The role of the teacher is to ask questions and create situations in which students are empowered to ask further questions.

ACTIVITY 4.4

> Suppose you are planning a unit of work on Sacred Texts. Suggest activities and/or questions you might include for each stage of the social constructivist approach outlined above.

Dialogical Approaches

The dialogical approach to religious education has been developed in England specifically in relation to the primary school context by Julia Ipgrave in the Institute of Education at the University of Warwick. Her focus was on multi-faith religious education, and in encouraging students to develop respect for those of different religious beliefs. The basis of the dialogical model is that students interpret and reinterpret their own views in the light of encounter with those who have different beliefs and values. When these different perspectives are brought together, the creation of new understandings and meanings may result (Ipgrave, 2005).

The process as outlined by Ipgrave involves the application of a three-fold understanding:

Primary Dialogue

- Acknowledging the diversity of experiences, viewpoints, understandings and ideas within the class.
- Using these as a resource for class discussions about beliefs and values.
- Introducing further viewpoints into classroom discussion.

For example, interviews could be set up with visitors from other faith communities, and through email partnership with students from different faith traditions in other schools. Discussion material on several religious traditions could be introduced.

Secondary Dialogue

- Promotes a class ethos in which children are willing to engage with difference, to share with and learn from others.
- Involving children in the establishment of principles for RE
- Encouraging questioning to develop interest in others' experiences and points of view.

For example, teaching the *skills* involved in listening to and learning from others, enabling the students themselves to discuss and set out the basic rules for the study of religion. Student themselves are encouraged to formulate their own questions when they engage with other religions and viewpoints. They are taught to try to view their own tradition from another's point of view. For example, Muslim children might be asked to watch a video of the hajj pilgrimage as though they were visiting from another planet, and to identify the elements they would find particularly strange and put together a list of questions they might ask.

Tertiary Dialogue

- Employing a variety of methods, strategies and exercises to facilitate dialogue in the school.
- Structuring activities that encourage students to express views, to negotiate and justify.
- Provide various stimuli to initiate and support discussion and debate (e.g., pictures, films, videos, case studies, stories, teachings from different traditions).

For example, students might engage in sorting exercises in which they classify or sequence cards with different statements, words, or pictures. As they do so they organize their thoughts, negotiate with each other, and justify their choices. Ipgrave (2005) recounts the class of eight year old children beginning a study of Islam who were asked to find different ways of completing the statement "a Muslim is someone who…". In groups they were required to choose four of these statements and record these onto cards. All the statements were then shared and classified under the headings "beliefs" and "practice" and then according to whether the statement applied only to Muslims or could also apply to various categories of non-Muslims. Also, role play could be used in which different groups or individuals have to argue a case from the point of view of a particular interest group.

Ipgrave (2005) notes that this dialogical approach could be adapted for use in other national or international contexts and could be employed in other curriculum fields such as intercultural education, education for democratic citizenship and human rights education.

ACTIVITY 4.5

Use the following PMI chart to outline the strengths and challenges of the Dialogical approach to multi-faith religious education:

Dialogical approach to multi-faith religious education		
Plus	Minus	Interesting

Conclusion

In this chapter we have explored some pertinent considerations in relation to contemporary multiculturalism and multi-faith religious education. Catering for such diversity in the religious education classroom can prove challenging for even the most experienced of religious educators. This is especially so in the Catholic primary/elementary school context, where in many instances multi-faith religious education is a missing component of the curriculum. The examples of multi-faith religious education presented in this chapter are certainly not exhaustive, and are in need of further development and adaptation. They do however serve to illustrate the possibilities which currently exist, as well as to stimulate further thought and discussion this area

Foster, C, (1991). Multicultural education: New directions for religious education. *PACE, 20*, 220-223.

Goldburg, P. (2007a). Study of religion as religious education in Catholic schools: A preliminary discussion. *Journal of Religious Education, 55* (1), 27-29.

Goldburg, P. (2007b). Broadening approaches to religious education through constructivist pedagogy. *Journal of Religious Education, 55* (2), 8-12.

Goosen, G. (1985). How multicultural is your RE classroom? *Journal of Christian Education*.

Grimmit, M. (2000). Constructivist pedagogies of religious education project: Re-thinking knowledge, teaching and learning religious education. In M. Grimmitt (Ed.), *Pedagogies of religious education: Case studies in the research and development of good pedagogic practice in RE* (pp. 207-227). Essex, UK: McCrimmons.

Healy, H., Hyde, B., & Rymarz, R. (2004). *Making our way through primary RE: A handbook for religious educators*. Tuggerah, NSW: Social Science Press.

Ipgrave, J. (2005). Pupil to pupil dialogue as a tool for religious education in the primary classroom. In R. Jackson & U. McKenna (Eds.). *Intercultural education and religious plurality* (pp. 39-42). Oslo, Norway: The Oslo Coalition on Freedom of Religion or Belief.

Jackson, R. (2005). Intercultural education, religious plurality and teaching for tolerance: Interpretive and dialogical approaches. In R. Jackson & U. McKenna (Eds.). *Intercultural education and religious plurality* (pp. 5-13). Oslo, Norway: The Oslo Coalition on Freedom of Religion or Belief.

Catholic Education Office, Melbourne. (1998). *To breathe again with two lungs.* Melbourne: Catholic Education Office.

CHAPTER 5

The Human, Cognitive, Faith, Moral and Spiritual Development of Students

One of the most important things to consider in Catholic school religious education is the way in which children develop as they grow and mature – cognitively morally, religiously and spiritually. For instance, an experienced practitioner of religious education would not teach using terms like "virtues", "faith", "hope" and "love" to students in the early years' classroom. These students would probably not as yet have developed the cognitive capacity to be able to understand these terms, nor the moral reasoning to enact these virtues. This is not to say that students in an early years' classroom are not active learners who are capable of a great many skills and abilities. We know that young students are highly capable learners who bring diverse and rich experiences to the classroom. But in order to align the planned learning and teaching experiences with the capabilities of the students, it is necessary to take into account the developmental theories which indicate the trajectories or paths and stages through which people develop.

In this chapter we investigate what is known about five particular areas of development – human, cognitive, moral, faith and spiritual. We also explore briefly a new and emerging theory which views development not as a linear trajectory, but rather as a dynamic process which is impacted upon by numerous factors. This theory is known as Dynamic Systems Theory.

Human Development

Human development has some pertinent insights to offer religious education. One theorist who has explored the area of human development was Abraham Maslow. He believed that many mistakes in understanding human nature had been made through a failure to view adulthood as a period of potential change and growth (Petersen, 1989). For example, while it may have been concluded that slaves were bequeath with 'slave-like' personalities because they fulfilled their roles as slaves efficiently, Maslow would have questioned whether they would have changed in character if they had been given the opportunity to exercise leadership and free choice. He believed that the need to grow towards the higher limits of human capacity was an inherent feature of humankind. He also felt that there were natural obstacles to growth which prevent people from achieving this, such as the desire for familiarity, and the lack of encouragement to guide growth.

Another important prerequisite for development, according to Maslow (1970), was the satisfaction, or gratification of human needs. To this end, Malsow offered a theory of human motivation relating to human growth based on the gratification of needs. He suggested a hierarchy of human needs which, according to his argument, corresponded to the growth and maturity of the human person. When basic needs are met, or gratified, such as physical needs – food, shelter, comfort, and the like – other higher and more complex needs would arise. He proposed the following five-level hierarchy of needs:

1. Physiological needs – hunger, thirst, warmth
2. Safety needs – the need to be safe, free from pain, danger and anxiety
3. Esteem – the need for recognition of worth by one's peers
4. Belongingness and love – the need for affection, the need to value and be valued as a part of a group, the need for respect, dignity and self-respect
5. Self-actualization – the need to develop one's potential, the need to place long-term benefits to self and others before short term pleasures, the need to develop a sense of priority among needs, the need to know "who am I?"

The lowest level of the hierarchy represents the basic requirements for survival – food, water, warmth, and the like. A person whose needs remain unmet at this level has no energy to spare for needs at higher levels. Similarly, it is necessary for the needs represented at each subsequent level of the hierarchy to be gratified before motivational attention can turn to the next level.

ACTIVITY 5.1

> What are some of the implications of Maslow's theory of human motivation for students in religious education in the Catholic school context?

Maslow's hierarchy of human needs has relevance for religious education. For instance, if we consider the second level, then the classroom environment must be one in which students feel safe and free from anxiety if effective learning is to take place – not only in religious education, but in every subject area. The learning experiences which are planned and provided must avoid placing students in positions in which they may feel anxious, afraid, or unsafe. This does not mean that the planned activities cannot be challenging for students. Rather, it implies that students need to be supported in their learning, and experience success for their efforts. This would be essential if higher needs in the third level of the hierarchy – esteem – and other subsequent levels are to be realized.

Cognitive Development

Cognitive psychology has been highly influential in teaching us about the way in which people develop, and the stages through which people pass as they grow and mature. In particular, cognitive psychology has been influential in the thinking of theorists who have proposed models of human, cognitive, moral and faith development. Some of these theorists and their models are presented and discussed later in this chapter with a focus on their application to religious education. For now, we will focus briefly on the theory proposed by one well known cognitive psychologist, whose work has been highly influential in education generally for well over 50 years.

Jean Piaget

French psychologist Jean Piaget explored and described hierarchically how people develop cognitively. He argued that intellectual development occurs through a series of stages which can be characterized by qualitatively discrete cognitive structures. This is often referred to as *structuralism*. At each stage, an individual develops an increasingly more sophisticated mental process, leading eventually to the acquisition of fully logical cognitive operations (McInerney & McInerney, 2006).

Each of the stages in Piaget's model of cognitive development is outlined in the table below.

Table 5.1: An outline of each stage in Piaget's model of cognitive development

Sensorimotor (birth to 2 years)
Child assimilates information to a limited array of sensory and motor schemes. Child responds to stimuli, but does not remember, plan or intend.
Preoperational (2 to 5 years)
Child begins to know things not only through their physical actions, but also symbolically. Language acquisition assists the ability to reason about the world and to begin to solve problems.
Concrete operations (7 to 12 years)
Child acquires and is capable of using a variety of logical operations to reason about the world and to solve problems, including the ability to classify, serialize and quantify objects. However, these operations are restricted to concrete (hands-on) experiences.
Formal operations (12 years onwards)
Emergence of the ability to think abstractly and in a scientific way. The formal patterns of thought which emerge include hypothetical reasoning, the ability to think propositionally, and combinatorial logic – the ability to take into account all possible combinations, or aspects of a problem without reference to physical reality.

ACTIVITY 5.2

> What are some of the implications of Piaget's model of cognitive development for students in religious education in the Catholic school context?

One of the clear implications of Piaget's model is that it would be inappropriate to introduce concepts that require abstract throught processes before students have progressed through the stages of cognitive development which precede the ability to deal with abstractions, such as the concrete-operational stage. This can be problematic when most Diocesan syllabi in religious education require, for example, the introduction of terms like "resurrection" when teaching about Easter. This raises serious questions in terms of the content which might be explored with younger students (see Grajczonek, 2005).

Another implication concerns the types of learning and teaching strategies and activities in religious education which are planned for students' engagement. For younger students, concrete materials and "hands-on" activities are more appropriate to enhance understanding. For older students, it may be more appropriate to include activities which require increasing opportunities for abstract thought.

Lev Vygotsky

Rather than focusing on cognitive structures, Russian psychologist Lev Vygotsky emphasized the cultural-historical aspects of cognitive development, in which learning is viewed as a process of appropriation by the child of culturally relevant behaviours. Vygotsky argued that learning is not a passive, solitary undertaking, but rather that it is a socially constructed activity. In other words, he placed an emphasis upon the role of the child's social and cultural world in their construction of meaning. Such a view is often referred to as *constructivism*, which views learning as an active process in which the learner constructs knowledge. According to Vygotsky's theory, children are born with a wide range of perceptual, attitudinal and memory capabilities which are substantially transformed in the context of socialization and education, particularly through social structure, language, and various "tools" to constitute the higher psychological functions or the unique forms of human cognition. Such "tools" could consist of pens, paintbrushes, calculators, and other various symbol systems, including language and mathematical notation. The social structures and language systems of the learners themselves are crucial in Vygotsky's theory. Learning develops then as a process through which the individual becomes one with the collective through carrying out personal activity in collaboration with others. For Vygotsky, cognitive development is not so much the expression of mental schemas within the individual (as in Piagetian theory), but rather the unfolding of cognitive understandings of social beings within social contexts. The individual becomes part of the community, and the community becomes part of the individual in the sharing and constructing of knowledge (McInerney & McInerney, 2006).

The social nature of learning is a feature of many school classrooms, particularly in the early years' of schooling. In such classrooms, students work together in small groups where interaction with other students is both valued and encouraged. Some writers have suggested that constructivist classrooms may be more effective in encouraging student's cognitive, social and moral development than are classrooms that employ more teacher-centered models (Gordon & Williams-Browne, 2000).

In constructivist models of learning, procedural knowledge, characterized by trial and error, copying by doing, and the like, is favored over factual knowledge. Activities indicative of procedural knowledge engage students in their learning, and might involve tasks like writing, devising, making, presenting, or even interviewing, rather than simply completing a series of questions on an activity sheet (Chase, 2000).

The notion of *scaffolding* is an important concept in Vygotsky's social constructivist theory. It places significance upon the role of the adults who provide support for students as they move to a higher level of performance in what Vygotsky termed the "zone of proximal development" (ZPD) (Williams, 1999). ZPD is a complex and debated concept. In essence it refers to a person's range of potential for learning. Vygotsky describes the ZPD as the distance between the actual developmental level of the child and the potential development as determined through problem-solving under the guidance of adults or in collaboration with more capable peers (McInerney & McInerney, 2006). To situate learning in the ZPD, an appropriate level of difficulty needs to be established. This must be challenging, but not too difficult. The educator then needs to provide guided practice to the student with a definite sense of the intended goal or outcome of the student's performance. This is referred to as "scaffolded instruction". As with scaffolding around a building, it is gradually removed so that, in time, the student can perform the task independently. If the learning experience has been carefully structured and situated within the student's ZPD, the student should, in time, be able to master the skill, or perform the task independently.

Scaffolding has a crucial role to play in religious education, where student's religious knowledge and understanding is often limited. The notion of scaffolding involves more than helping students to solve problems. It entails being able to provide appropriate resources and materials to support students in their learning. For example, in learning about the Eucharist in religious education, scaffolding might include providing labelled photos or illustrations of the altar, the lectern, and the different vessels which are used – chalice, ciborium, cruets, and the like. Scaffolding requires religious educators to be aware of students' needs in terms of concepts, language, and experiences. It involves "being in tune with [students'] thinking and being ready to step in at opportune times to supply the missing piece of information…or to ask the right question that guides children to further learning without taking over" (Grajczonek, 2004, p. 54).

Moral Development

Greatly influenced by Piaget and the notion of hierarchical stages through which people pass in cognitive development generally, Lawrence Kohlberg proposed a theory which sought to identify how an individual might develop morally. He proposed that people mature in their moral reasoning by passing through a number of levels, each characterized by qualitatively discrete structures. Each of these levels is recognized by the **reasons** that are given by a person for choosing between right and wrong. In other words, a level of reasoning is not decided by the actions that may be considered to be wrong, but rather by the reasons given that determine whether the action is wrong. Kohlberg described three levels, each of which has two stages, as outlined in the Table 5.2.

Table 5.2: An outline of each stage in Kohlberg's theory of moral development

Level	Description
Pre-conventional Level	
1. Orientation towards punishment	A person is deterred from doing something wrong because of the consequences that might occur.
2. Reciprocity	A right action is when one seeks to satisfy one's own needs, and occasionally the needs of others.
Conventional Level	
3. Good boy-good girl orientation	A person seeks the approval of others for good behavior.
4. Orientation towards authority	Doing one's duty, showing respect for authority and maintaining the social order determines the right behavior
Post-conventional Level	
5. Social contract orientation	The right action is determined by standards that have been accepted and agreed upon by the community
6. Universal ethical principal orientation	An orientation towards decisions of conscience and toward self-chosen ethical principles that relate to justice, equity, human dignity, etc

ACTIVITY 5.3

What are some of the implications of Kohlberg's theory of moral development for students in religious education in the Catholic school context?

Kohlberg's model has assisted religious educators in understanding the reasoning structures which influence people as they discern solutions to moral dilemmas. Many of the syllabi and Diocesan documents and guidelines on religious education have been influenced by this model.

However, some theorists have been critical. For instance, some have argued that Kohlberg's research (which led to the development of his model) was dominated by an all-male sample and that the post-conventional levels for female moral development were not examined. Others have maintained that Kohlberg's model reduced the study of moral concepts to the study of verbal justification of moral ideas. Moral understandings had been narrowed to the study of what a person could propositionalize. Still others have argued that Kohlberg's model failed to take in to account the role of the emotions as an essential element in moral development. As well, there is serious doubt among scholars as to whether Kohlberg's model could be said to have universal application. While certain behaviours may be considered as right or wrong regardless of the laws and practices of different cultures, some moral values, such as equality, freedom, and the like are not so universally applied across cultural boundaries. Given the pluralistic nature of many religious education classrooms in western culture, religious educators would need to be aware of these implications when planning and developing aspects of moral education programs.

Faith Development

Having been influenced by the structural developmental psychologists such as Piaget and Kohlberg, theorist James Fowler researched the notion of faith and how faith might be understood to develop across the lifespan of a person. Fowler's (1981) understanding of faith is interesting because it differs from that of other theorists who have an interest in this area. For Fowler, faith is a universal. It is something which all people have, for example, faith in a cause beyond themselves. It is concerned with more than belief in a particular religious tradition. For Fowler, faith concerns the process of meaning making – a process in which all human beings engage. Fowler believes that the process of meaning making develops in predictable stages which are linked to chronological age. In drawing on the theories of structural-developmental psychology Fowler maintains that each stage of faith broadly corresponds to the development in thinking capacities of people.

Fowler proposes six stages of faith in addition to a "pre-stage", which he terms as primal faith. Each of these is briefly summarized in Table 5.3 below.

Table 5.3: An outline of each stage in Fowler's theory of faith development

Pre-stage: Primal faith (infancy)
Faith gained from parents and care-givers. Generally experiences of trust
Stage 1: Intuitive-projective faith (early childhood)
Young children copy the language and actions of adults close to them
Stage 2: Mythic-literal faith (childhood and beyond)
Older children begin to express beliefs that they have heard and begin to act upon them
Stage 3: Synthetic-conventional faith (adolescence and beyond)
Children in their teenage years begin to be influenced by a wider network including their peers
Stage 4: Individuative-reflective faith (young adulthood and beyond)
Tension is experience between choosing to stay with the known and familiar, or developing one's own individuality and exploring unknown territory. Fowler claims this latter step is necessary for faith to continue to develop
Stage 5: Conjunctive faith (early mid-life and beyond)
The individual chooses to live according to her or his own beliefs and commitments
Stage 6: Universalizing faith (mid-life and beyond)
The individual focuses on truths and what it means to be human. The person is comfortable with her or his own beliefs and could develop a commitment to change the world

Fowler did attempt to link specific age periods with each of the six stages but conceded that stage attainment would vary from person to person. More importantly, he maintained that only a few individuals would reach the sixth and final stage, for instance, people like Mother Theresa, or Gandhi.

ACTIVITY 5.4

> Consider the stages of faith development which are most pertinent to students in the Catholic schools. What are some of the implications of these stages for religious education?

The theory of faith development proposed by Fowler has attracted both support and criticism. Those who have interests in nurturing faith have praised Fowler's work for the insights it brings to the process of faith sharing. However, Fowler's concern is with *how* a person believes (the process) rather than *what* a person believes (the content). Those who criticize Fowler's model argue that it is therefore difficult to distinguish between the faith of a religious believer, an atheist, and a humanist, since according to Fowler, all have faith and can be potentially found at all stages. Others have argued that the influence of cognitive development in Fowler's model has rendered faith as a type of knowing, with little attention given to the role of feelings and values, which are inextricably infused in faith.

Spiritual Development

Another area of development which is of concern to religious educators is spiritual development. Since the word "spirituality" has come to mean different things to different people, it is important to begin by describing briefly the meaning this word has in this chapter.

Describing spirituality

Much of the contemporary research suggests that spirituality is concerned with a person's sense of connectedness or relationship with self, others, the world (or indeed the cosmos) and for many, with a Transcendent dimension – God in the Christian tradition. Hay and Nye's (2006) study with children in Britain suggested that at the core of children's spirituality was what they have termed "relational consciousness" – a conscious awareness of their sense of relationship with themselves and with everything other than themselves. Spirituality is a natural human predisposition. It is a quality that all human beings possess, regardless of whether or not they belong to, or practice, a particular religious tradition. Therefore, spirituality and religion are not the same thing, although a person's spirituality may be given expression through a religious tradition. So, regardless of a person's affiliation with religion, spirituality is expressed outwardly in terms of the relationships people have with the human and non-human world. Since spirituality is primarily concerned with the idea of relationship, and that could include a relationship with God, it is something that religious educators are particularly interested in, and something that they may seek to nurture through the classroom RE program.

Spiritual development or spiritual integration?

There is plenty of research which attests to the existence of a spiritual dimension to the lives of children and young people (e.g., Adams, Hyde & Woolley, 2008; Champagne, 2001; de Souza, 2006; Hart, 2003; Hyde, 2008). Table 5.4 below briefly outlines some of the key findings from contemporary research which attest to the spiritual dimension of children's lives.

There is however, some question as to whether children actually *develop* spiritually, at least in a Piagetian sense. That is, many theorists have questioned whether in fact children develop spiritually in the same way that we think of them developing physically, or intellectually. In fact Eaude (2005) and Priestley (2000) argue that children have qualities and features which seem to be lost or suppressed as they get older. In some areas, such as moral judgment, children may develop. However, in others, such as the capacity for joy or curiosity, they seem to have something which adults loose. This may accord with how many religious traditions regard children as having access to a profound spirituality.

Table 5.4: A summary of findings from contemporary research attesting to the spiritual dimension of children's lives

Champagne (2001)	Hart (2003)	Hyde (2008)	Adams, Hyde & Woolley (2008)
Listening to and listening for spirituality Three insights: • Spiritual experience is human experience • Ordinary, everyday experiences of children may be spiritual • The importance of adults to see children as having agency	Five spiritual capacities in children: • Wisdom • Wonder/Awe • Between You and Me • Seeing the invisible • Wondering (about existential questions)	Four characteristics of children's spirituality: • The felt sense • Integrating awareness • Weaving the threads of meaning • Spiritual questing	Key issue surrounding spirituality and its continual expression in children: • The voice of the child • Children's experiences – ordinary and extraordinary • The significance of children's contexts • Acknowledging the worldviews of children • Making meaning from children's dreams

Hay and Nye (2006) suggest that as children get older, their spirituality is suppressed or overlaid by the processes of socialization that prevail in western culture. It is not common for people to discuss spiritual matters or express a sense of wonder and awe in relation to everyday occurrences. They tend to keep these private. As children grow older, they become socialized into a culture that relegates the spiritual to the private and often unacknowledged domain of the person. Hay and Nye argue that this discarding of the spiritual is not a natural phenomenon. It is the task of educators generally to nurture and protect this dimension of children's lives. Religious educators have a particular role to play here. The role of the teacher becomes one of reconstructing a climate in which spirituality is nourished.

Rather than spiritual development, Eaude (2005) suggests the terms could be re-envisioned as *spiritual integration*. The notion of integration implies that a person can regress as well as progress. If children do possess capacities such as openness, curiosity and joy, the teacher must allow and enable these to flourish. In this way spirituality is nurtured. Eaude (2005) and Hyde (2008) suggest that activities already familiar to most classroom teachers can contribute to and nurture spirituality. It does not entail developing anything new – merely recognizing the opportunities that activities which already form part of the curriculum may have in nurturing spirituality.

Dynamic Systems Theory

As can be seen above, there is some debate as to whether children develop spiritually – at least when considering traditional models of development. One of the main criticisms – and limitations – of developmental theories is that they assume the development of a person follows a continuous straight or curved trajectory. In other words, these models understand development to be *linear*. If there are variations in a person's development, they are often assumed to reflect random fluctuations or errors in measurement. Contemporary research understands the development of a person in any dimension to be far more complex, often involving regression as well as progression. It is in relation to this that the notion of *Dynamic Systems Theory* (DST) has been proposed particularly in relation to spiritual development (Cupit, 2005, 2007), but can be applied to development more generally. DST claims to takes account of the full complexity of developing human "systems". It is not an easy theory to characterize, and this is exacerbated by the subject specific terminology which accompanies this theory – terms like "chaos", "butterfly effect", "attractors", and "structural conspiracies", to name but a few. And although the theory is far too complex to describe in one chapter, there are nine key principles which underpin the theory, and which have possible relevance for religious educators. Each of these is explored below.

Principle 1: Persistent pressure to change

Development is driven by a variety of features of the world in which children live. Everything that energies and feeds energy or information to them drives children to develop. These can include the process of maturation – the impetus to grow which is "built into" children's genes, as well as environmental features to which children may be exposed and from which they learn. All of these features result in a constant pressure on children (and adults for that matter) to change and to develop.

ACTIVITY 5.5

> List and discuss 3 possible factors which might result pressure to change.

Principle 2: Resistance to change

Although there is pressure to grow and to develop, there is also resistance to change. Children can settle into particular patterns of thinking, feeling and behaving which can be so stable that, for a time, they will resist influences that promote change. For example, a toddler may insist on drinking from her or his bottle, even though she or he has been taught to use a cup. Similarly, a child of school age may resist effort to curb disruptive behaviour. These stable patterns are called *attractors* because children are attracted into them (Cupit, 2005).

Attractors are a crucial factor in development. They are not predictable from anything in children's biology, nor from anything in their previous history, but they seem to be shared by all children. They are common patterns which each child expresses in their own unique way (Cupit, 2005).

ACTIVITY 5.6

> What kinds of behaviour patterns might be considered as possible attractors – stable behaviour patterns – to which children might be attracted?

Principle 3: Sudden major changes

Children's attractors are always under pressure to change. For example, a parent will continue to offer a cup to the toddler rather than a bottle. Teachers continue to tell a child that their behaviour is unacceptable. This results in children's behaviour drifting into what is referred to a chaos (Cupit, 2005). This is where, for example, the toddler unpredictably demands a bottle at times, and a cup at other times. Eventually the child shifts to a radically new pattern or attractor – a new level of stability which in turn resists change.

The shift from one stable pattern of behaviour to another is always sudden and significant, rather than gradual or trivial. A stable phase gives way to a brief period of chaotic behaviour before a new and different stable phase emerges. "Sudden" developmental transitions may actually take months, but they are always brief as compared to the stable periods.

And, in some instances, previous patterns of behaviour do not completely disappear, but are retained within the new more capable system which emerges. For example, even though a child goes through a change which allows her or him to walk, the child may still choose to crawl.

Principle 4: Alternative attractors and individual trajectories (pathways)

As they mature, children are always confronted by alternatives from which to choose, in terms of behaviour, preferences, patterns of development, and the like. While many children may follow similar general patterns, and exhibit similar attractors, children (and adults for that matter) are able to choose alternative and individual pathways. While it might be possible to describe a child's "typical" form, no one child's pathway is ever exactly typical.

Principle 5: Sensitivity to small differences

In a dynamic system, very small changes can have major impacts (Cupit, 2005). Variations in children's experiences which may be barely discernable can result in children following quite different developmental pathways. One child might, for example, refuse to breast feed after being presented with the bottled alternative, while another child might resist weaning. An older sibling might call her or his parents by their first name, while a younger sibling, despite the model being presented, might insist on "mum" or "dad". Children's spiritual development in particular can be highly sensitive to small changes in their circumstances.

ACTIVITY 5.7

> Can you think of any other small changes which may have a major impact on a child's developmental pathway?

Principle 6: Agency

Children are agents who affect their own development. The conscious choices they make initiate, shape, and in some instances, limit their physical, psychological and other forms of development. Children are not machines which have been programmed to act and behave in certain ways. They are free to influence what they become. This is an important principle which is often overlooked in developmental theories. Even very young children have, and exercise, agency.

Principle 7: Entrainment

Although children (as well as adults) are subject to what their bodies and their personalities require of them, their spirit is able, within limits, to over-ride both body and character. Ordinarily a person eats when she or he is hungry, but a person can choose to fast. An individual's personality may tend to outbursts of anger, yet over time, that individual may learn to curb this excess. The "whole" of who a person is – the spirit – can over-rule the individual parts which make up the person, so that the physical and psychological parts fall into line. This process, in which the "whole" determines what the parts will do is called *entrainment* (Cupit, 2005).

In human beings, the decisions of the whole person influence the behaviour of the parts. At the same time, the parts are able to act independently and sometime shape what the whole requires. A person may feel hungry, but can choose to ignore the signals coming from the digestive system until it is convenient to eat. This might occur when a person chooses to wait to eat, even though hungry, so that she or he can eat with family or friends. Cupit (2005) notes that although children's spirits may be less able to command body and mind than are adults, children are nonetheless becoming more increasingly able.

ACTIVITY 5.8

> List and discuss 2 other examples of entrainment.

Principle 8: Individual expression of general patterns

Although being unique in detail, there is no doubt that children's development in various areas follows some shared general patterns. However, these similar patterns are expressed in unique ways in different children. Every child is unique and just how each pattern plays out with individual children is entirely unpredictable. Let's consider a batsman in the game of cricket as an example. Every batsman does exactly the same thing (that it, swinging the bat so as to hit the ball). But how each batsman does it is different and recognizably his own. So, while it is possible to draw general conclusions about the trajectories children may follow because of these common patterns, it is important to remember that each child's developmental pathway is unique, and can never be predicted in detail.

Principle 9: Emergence

In dynamic systems entirely new capacities "emerge". Cupit (2005) describes "emergence" as the appearance of something entirely new and unpredictably novel. It is not simply the further development of something that already exists. The most obvious example of this occurs at birth. As well, there are important transitions with the emergence of language. Another shift is the emergence of the ability to be critical about what children are told to believe and do. The next significant shift is signaled by the emergence of the ability of children to formulate and maintain their own stance on important matters. A final emergence is the ability to identify with particular spiritual paths and to effectively resist involvement with alternatives.

ACTIVITY 5.9

What might be some of the possible implications of DST for religious education?

Conclusion

As can be seen from this chapter, children and young people's human, cognitive, moral, faith and spiritual development is a complex process. While each of the theories which are based on cognitive development shed some light upon this developmental process, each is incomplete and, to a large extent, limited. They assume developmental pathways to proceed in linear ways. For some time now, educators generally have raised questions in relation to these theories. They do not seem to adequately account for the differences and variation in the ways in which children and young people develop.

Dynamic systems theory offers an alternative. Although it is difficult to characterize, it certainly demonstrates that the development of the individual is complex, and cannot be explained adequately by traditional cognitive theories of development. Development is a dynamic process which is impacted upon by numerous factors. While it is not intended that religious educators become experts in this area, it is important that religious educators acknowledge the complexity of their students' development, and perhaps consider how the various principles of DST might influence their planning and classroom practice.

Adams, K., Hyde, B. & Woolley, R. (2008). *The spiritual dimension of childhood*. London: Jessica Kingsley.

Champagne, E. (2001). Listening to…listening for…: A theological reflection on spirituality in early childhood. In J. Erricker, C. Ota, and C. Erricker (Eds.), *Spiritual education. Cultural, religious and social differences: New perspectives for the 21st century* (pp. 76-87). Brighton: Sussex Academic.

Chase, L. (2000). Language development. In D. Dixon & K. Goold (Eds.), *Extending child development from five to twelve years* (pp. 79-99). Katoomba, NSW: Social Science Press.

Cupit, G. (2005). *Perspectives on children and spirituality*. Newcastle, NSW: Scripture Union Australia).

Cupit, G. (2007). The marriage of science and spirit: Dynamic systems theory and the development of spirituality. *International Journal of Children's Spirituality, 12* (2), 105-116.

Eaude, T. (2005). Strangely familiar? – Teachers making sense of young children's spiritual development. *Early years, 25* (3), 237-248.

Fowler, J. (1981). *Stages of faith: The psychology of human development and the quest for meaning*. Blackburn, VIC: Collins Dove.

Gordon, A., & Williams-Browne, K. (2000). *Beginnings and beyond* (5th ed.). Australia: Delmar Thomson Learning.

Grajczonek, J. (2004). Stop, look and learn: Re-visioning pedagogy in early years' religion settings. *Journal of Religious Education, 52* (3), 52-59.

Grajczonek, J. (2005). Integration, insight and implications: Recognizing the dilemmas of early childhood religious education. *Journal of Religious Education, 53* (3), 43-56.

Hart, T. (2003). *The secret spiritual world of children*. Makawao, HI: Inner Ocean.

Hay, D., & Nye, R. (2006). *The spirit of the child* (rev. ed). London: Jessica Kingsley.

Hyde, B. (2008). *Children and spirituality: Searching for meaning and connectedness*. London: Jessica Kingsley.

Kohlberg, L. (1981). *The philosophy of moral development*. San Francisco: Harper & Row.

Petersen, C. (1989). *Looking forward through the lifespan*. New York: Prentice Hall.

Piaget, J. (1971). *The children's conception of the world* (trans. by J. Tomlinson & A. Tomlinson). London: Routledge & Kegan Paul.

Priestley, J. (2000). Moral and spiritual growth. In J. Mills & R. Mills (Eds.), *Childhood studies: A reader in perspectives of childhood* (pp. 113-128). London: Routledge.

Maslow, A. (1970). *Motivation and personality* (2nd ed). New York: Harper & Row.

McInerney, D., & McInerney, V. (2006). *Educational psychology: Constructing learning*. Frenchs Forest, NSW: Pearson Prentice Hall.

Vygotsky, L. (1987). *Thinking and speech* (ed. & trans. By N. Minick). New York: Plenum Press.

CHAPTER 6

The Perceiving, Thinking, Feeling and Intuiting Elements in the Learning Process

A scenario

Aaron is a Grade 5 teachers. The students in his class are around 10 years of age. As a part of a unit of work focusing on The Eucharist, Aaron has planned a lesson in which he introduces students to the four ways in which Jesus is present in the Eucharist – in the gathered assembly, in the priest who acts in the name of Jesus, in the Word proclaimed, and most especially in the Eucharistic species (the bread and wine which will become the Body and Blood of Christ). Aaron's lesson is well structured. His cognitive outcome is clearly stated: That by the end of the lesson, students will be able to name the four ways in which Jesus is present in the Eucharist. As well, Aaron has planned an appropriate assessment task which will enable him to collect evidence of students having achieved the outcome. He begins with some questions designed to enable students to recall the focus of the previous lesson. He introduces the new content by showing the students some photographs of the people who have gathered for a Sunday Mass, the priest, someone reading one of the readings, and the consecration of the bread and wine. However, while Aaron is showing the class each picture, being careful to maintain eye contact with his students, he notices that many of them are starring at the photographs as though they are totally unfamiliar with the content of them. Next, he asks the students to get their copy of the diocesan approved text book, and to turn to page 57, where there is a short explanation for the four ways in which Jesus is present in the Eucharist. They do this obediently. Aaron asks the students to record, in pairs, any vocabulary in the text with which they are not familiar. Many of the students compile quite lengthy lists. Finally, Aaron asks his students to take a piece of paper, fold it into four equal parts, and in each quadrant, to draw or depict one of the four ways in which Jesus is present in the Eucharist (the assessment task). Most of the students seem to be able to do this. In his evaluation, Aaron notes that although students seemed to complete the assessment task, many were scratching their heads as if in confusion, or starring vaguely at the photographs he had shown them. Although he is not sure what, Aaron suspects that something in his lesson was not effective.

Aaron's concerns are confirmed the following day. At the beginning of the religious education session, he asks his students to recap what they had covered in the last session. The students stare blankly at him. Not one can recall the content of the previous lesson.

ACTIVITY 6.1

With a partner, discuss what seems to have happened in the above scenario. Can you see anything missing in Aaron's approach to RE in this topic? Why do you think the students were unable to recall the content of the previous lesson? What might you do differently?

The above scenario suggests that, although much work has been done in the area of curriculum development in religious education, effective learning and teaching does not always result. In recent times, pedagogical practice in education in western civilization generally is represented by outcomes based approaches to the curriculum. You would have noticed that Aaron in the above scenario has an outcome for his lesson. Rather than focusing on the content, outcomes based approaches focus on the knowledge, skills, and understandings which students are expected to acquire. This sounds reasonable. So, why were the students in Aaron's class unable to make meaning from the material presented, and unable to recall it the following day? Could it be that the learning model used by Aaron in that particular lesson was limited in effectively engaging the students and in promoting learning?

One of the criticisms of the outcomes based approach to education is that it does not take adequate account of other dimensions in which students learn. These are often referred to as the *non-cognitive* dimensions. In particular, these include (but are not limited to) the affective and spiritual dimensions. Aaron's lesson above had a clear focus on the cognitive dimension of learning, although it seems that little attention was explicitly paid to those other ways in which students learn. Research has shown that it is often through the non-cognitive dimensions of learning that students not only learn and achieve outcomes, but are *engaged* in learning. Perhaps here is the clue Aaron would be looking for: his students were not engaged in their learning. If they were, they would have been able to easily recall the material of the previous lesson. There is a need at the present time for professional learning programs for teachers in which appropriate learning models are explored that may enable them to develop new perspectives about engaging students by incorporating different aspects of learning. In this chapter, we explore one such model which incorporates some of these aspects of learning: cognitive, affective, and spiritual; and the associated processes – perceiving, thinking, feeling and intuiting. The work of Australian scholar Marian de Souza will be drawn upon here. Her work provides one example of an appropriate learning model which addresses these aspects of learning. This particular model focuses on the integration of the cognitive, affective and spiritual dimensions of learning, and on the associated processes – perceiving, thinking, feeling and intuiting.

Perceiving

To perceive means to become aware of something through the senses of seeing, hearing, touching, smelling, and tasting. It also means to comprehend – that is, to understand, or to make meaning of something through the senses. This is the first of the elements associated with de Souza's (2004, 2006) model. In terms of the learning process, a person first begins to learn about something by consciously perceiving through the senses. For example, a small child first learns about the delights of ice cream through the sense of taste. An adult may begin to learn about the detrimental effects of smoking by seeing what prolonged smoking does to the health of a person. Some recent advertisements of television have been effective here. A student may begin to learn about the concept of pitch in music through hearing. In other words, learning begins with a person sensing and perceiving an aspect of the outer world – the world which presents itself to the student. In the classroom, this world may include the presentation of particular material pertaining to a particular subject area by the teacher. It also includes the physical classroom environment and ambiance, both of which are perceived by students in sensorial ways.

ACTIVITY 6.2

> In the religious education classroom, what kinds of stimuli might be perceived, or sensed, by the students? Discuss your response with a partner.

Thinking

Once something from the outer world has been perceived or sensed by students, it effectually enters the inner world of the students, where two other processes become active. One of these is the thinking process. The thinking process represents the intellectual or *cognitive* dimension. Psychologists have used the term "intelligence" to speak about this process. It has a particular focus on the ability to solve problems and to think in an abstract fashion (Chui, Hong, & Dweck, 1994; Mayer, 2000). Some psychologists, such as Howard Gardner, have argued in favour of multiple intellectual capacities, hence the term "multiple intelligences" (Gardner, 1993). The notion of intelligence represents the cognitive dimension of learning and is concerned with the acquisition of knowledge, skills, abilities and understandings.

ACTIVITY 6.3

> Make a list of some of the knowledge, skills and understandings students might be required to master in a religious education program.

When something is perceived by students from the outer world, one of the first things a student does is to think about what has been perceived. For example, a student who hears a question raised by the class teacher immediately begins to think about the question in terms of an appropriate response which might be given. A driver who experiences a problem with the engine opens the hood of the car to see whether there is anything that can be done to solve the problem.

Often this is the process given most attention by outcomes based approaches to education. Learning rarely moves beyond this point. However, students seldom learn solely through the thinking process (the cognitive dimension), and many have argued that cognitive knowledge by itself is insufficient to ensure that genuine learning has taken place (see for example Buchanan & Hyde, 2008). Learning has to *affect* the student.

Feeling

The second of the two processes which becomes active when stimuli from the outer world enter the inner world of the student is the feeling process. The importance of the feeling process – the *affective* dimension – has been attested to in recent literature which has explored the concept of *emotional intelligence (EQ – emotional quotient)*, particularly by Goleman (1995) and by Mayer, Salovey and Caruso (2000). Emotional intelligence is described as the ability to process emotional information, particularly as it involves perception, assimilation, and the understanding and management of emotion, that is, the capacity to carry out abstract reasoning, which is a hallmark of intelligence.

Goleman (1995) argued that cognitive intelligence (IQ) and emotional intelligence (EQ) are not opposing competencies. "These two minds, the emotional and the rational, operate in tight harmony for the most part, intertwining their very different ways of knowing to guide us through the world" (p. 9). He also argued that one's emotional intelligence is a fundamental requirement for one's effective use of rational intelligence. In other words, a person's feelings play an important role in their thought process (Hyde, 2003). Consequently, recognizing the role of the emotions in the intellectual performance and life of a student should be an important factor in the learning process.

When something is perceived by students from the outer world, as well as thinking logically about what has been perceived, a student might also develop feelings about what has been perceived, make value judgments and form views about it. For example, a student might see some video footage of children suffering in a third world country, and develop particular emotions in relation to the image, or even make moral judgments which question how such poverty might be allowed to exist. Similarly, a driver, who sees an advertisement on television warning about the dangers of speeding, could express an emotional response to the images shown. In these instances, both the thinking and feeling processes are at work. It is important to note that the thinking and feeling process work together. They are interdependent. It is also worth noting that in many instances, once something from the outer world has been perceived, that it could well be the feeling process which is first activated. For example, a person who hears a beautiful piece of music may have an emotional reaction to it before beginning to think about it. In any case, it has been argued that the activation of both of these processes may result in a greater engagement on the part of the student, and ultimately, in longer lasting learning.

ACTIVITY 6.4

> What words would you use to describe the kinds of feelings or reaction students might experience in relation to what they perceive in the religious education classroom? Make a list and compare with a partner.

Intuiting (the Spiritual Dimension)

The process of intuiting pertains to the inner life. The notion of spiritual intelligence (SQ) as proposed in particular by Zohar and Marshall (2000) captures something of this process. Spiritual intelligence is necessary for the effective functioning of both cognitive and emotional intelligence, since "neither IQ nor EQ, separately or in combination, is enough to explain the full complexity of human intelligence nor the vast richness of the human soul and imagination" (Zohar & Marshall, 2000, p. 5). According to these writers spiritual intelligence is the function which integrates cognition and feeling, and places one's life into a richer meaning-making context. It has to do with the *relational* component to one's life. The *spiritual dimension* is therefore a vital factor in a person's life, and one which cannot be ignored in the learning process.

The work of theorists such as O'Connor (1990) and Claxton (2003) suggest that intuition is a different way of knowing. Intuition pertains to inner life and experience. It is the function that informs people about the atmosphere that surrounds an event or an experience. It is the function that presents future possibilities. In drawing on the work of all of these writers, de Souza (2004) argues that intuition is activated when new thoughts and feelings, which have been provoked by perceptions or sensations from the outer world, become absorbed and stored at the depth level – the core of a person's being. The new learning which emanates from this merging of thinking and feeling may translate into changed attitudes and/or behaviour – that is, the relational, or spiritual dimension. In this way, de Souza argues that learning may be transformational when it results from an integration of the four elements of perceiving, thinking, feeling and intuiting. Without such integration it is possible that learning may remain at a superficial level, where it does not touch the student's inner being.

Perhaps this is what was missing from Aaron's lesson at the beginning of the chapter. The learning remained at a superficial level and was not remembered by the students in subsequent lessons. The learning may have engaged students' thinking, but the other processes of feeling and intuiting were not involved, and thus did not integrate with the thinking process.

de Souza (2006) subsequently proposes that the concepts of cognitive, emotional and spiritual intelligence may provide a useful framework for the learning and teaching process so that cognitive and affective learning might be complimented by spiritual learning. To this end, de Souza has proposed a model which recognizes the complementarity of these intelligences, and the associated processes of perceiving, thinking, feeling and intuiting. The interaction and integration of these may lead to a depth of learning which has the potential to be transformational.

Figure 6.1: A curriculum model: the learning process – intuiting, thinking, feeling, intuiting

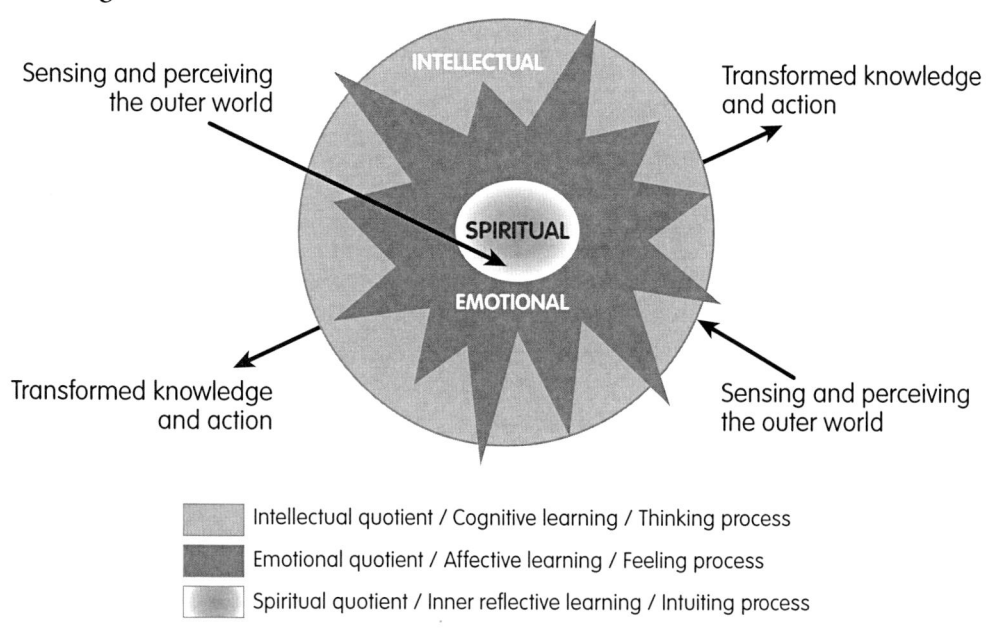

Sensing and perceiving the outer world

Transformed knowledge and action

INTELLECTUAL

SPIRITUAL

EMOTIONAL

Transformed knowledge and action

Sensing and perceiving the outer world

- Intellectual quotient / Cognitive learning / Thinking process
- Emotional quotient / Affective learning / Feeling process
- Spiritual quotient / Inner reflective learning / Intuiting process

In order to apply this model of learning in education (an in religious education in particular) learning outcomes for each of the three dimensions – cognitive, affective and spiritual – need to be articulated (given the outcomes based focus on curriculum at the present time). While cognitive outcomes are articulated as specific learning that will be demonstrated at the end of a unit of work, the proposed affective and spiritual outcomes are expressed as hoped-for outcomes. Affective outcomes may not become evident in the space available for one lesson, or even a whole unit of work. The spiritual outcomes indicate the shift that may take place within the student at a depth level. This may involve a corresponding change in thinking and behaviour patterns which can only occur after a period of time. Nonetheless, it should be factored into teachers' planning so that opportunities are offered for students to develop these aspects of learning.

The following is indicative of a cognitive outcome:

> By the end of this lesson (or unit) students will be able to distinguish between a parable and a miracle story in the Gospel of Luke by identifying two features of these literary forms.

Buchanan & Hyde (2008)

An affective outcome could be:

> By the end of this unit of work students will have an opportunity to appreciate the way Jesus used parables to teach people about God.

Buchanan & Hyde (2008)

An example of a spiritual outcome could be:
> By the end of this unit of work students will have the opportunity to reflect inwardly on the message of one parable to consider how the message might challenge their present behaviour.

ACTIVITY 6.5
> Suppose that you are planning a unit of work which focuses on the Sacrament of Penance (Reconciliation). With a partner, devise one possible cognitive, affective and spiritual outcome which might be included in this unit.

While affective and spiritual outcome statements may not be demonstrable or measurable, they do help to ensure that teachers keep these three aspects of learning in mind as they plan and teach. As de Souza (2006) and Buchanan and Hyde (2008) have argued, this reduces that chance that learning will remain at the surface and cognitive levels. The inclusion of these dimensions is an educative means which has the potential to lead to transformative learning experiences which may provide a more lasting impact upon the learners.

ACTIVITY 6.6
> Plan two or three possible learning and teaching experiences that you would include in the above unit of work on the Sacrament of Penance (Reconciliation) which address the cognitive, affective and spiritual dimensions. Can you devise one activity which potentially addresses all three dimensions (and hence, all three outcomes)?

Conclusion

If learners are to achieve not only the cognitive competencies that comprise the religious education curriculum (or indeed, any given curriculum area), but engage in the type of learning experiences which have the power to be transformative – when learning goes beyond to surface and touches the soul of the student (de Souza, 2006), leading the individual to act upon what has been learned – then a more holistic pedagogical approach is required. The learning model presented in this chapter is one which represents a conscious effort to give adequate attention to the cognitive, affective and spiritual dimensions of learning, and to the associated processes of perceiving (or sensing), thinking, feeling and intuiting.

Buchanan, M. & Hyde, B. (2008). Learning beyond the surface: Engaging the cognitive, affective and spiritual dimensions within the curriculum. *International Journal of Children's Spirituality, 13* (4), 309-320.

Chiu, C., Hong, Y. & Dweck, C. (1994). Towards an integrative model of personality and intelligence: A general framework and some preliminary steps. In R. Sternberg & P. Ruzgis (Eds.), *Personality and intelligence* (pp. 104-134). New York: Cambridge University Press.

Claxton, G. (2000). The anatomy of intuition. In T. Atkinson & G. Claxton (Eds.), *The intuitive practitioner: On the value of not always knowing what one is doing.* Buckingham, Philadelphia: Open University Press.

de Souza, M. (2004). Teaching for effective learning in religious education: A discussion of the perceiving, thinking, feeling and intuiting elements in the learning process. *Journal of Religious Education, 52* (3), 22-30.

de Souza, M. (2006). Rediscovering the spiritual dimension in education: Promoting a sense of self and place, meaning and purpose in learning. In M. de Souza, K. Engebretson, G. Durka, R. Jackson, & A. McGrady (Eds.). *International handbook of the religious, moral and spiritual dimensions in education* (pp. 1127-1139). AA Dordrecht, The Netherlands: Springer.

Gardner, H. (1993). *Multiple intelligences: The theory in practice.* New York: Basic Books.

Goleman, D. (1995). *Emotional intelligence: Why it can matter more than IQ.* London: Bloomsbury.

Hyde, B. (2003). Spiritual intelligence: A critique. *Journal of Religious Education, 51* (1), 13-20.

Mayer, J. (2000). Spiritual intelligence or spiritual consciousness? *The International Journal for the Psychology of Religion, 50* (1), 47-56.

Mayer, J., Salovey, P., & Caruso, D. (2000). Models of emotional intelligence. In R. Sternberg (Ed.), *Handbook of intelligence* (pp. 396-420). Cambridge, UK: Cambridge University Press.

O'Connor, P. (1990). *Understanding Jung.* Port Melbourne, VIC: Mandarin.

Zohar, D., & Marshall, I. (2000). *SQ. Spiritual intelligence: The ultimate intelligence.* London: Bloomsbury.

PART 2
Pedagogical Considerations

CHAPTER 7

The Content of the Religious Education Syllabus

In this chapter we examine broadly the content that is taught in the religious education program in Catholic schools. While Catholic schools generally arrange the RE curriculum through programming and planning for learning and teaching at whole school and the individual classroom levels, the syllabus for programming and planning is devised by curriculum planners, positions often held, in this instance, by personnel in local Catholic Education Offices. However, it is the Archbishop, or diocesan Bishop, in his role as the principal teacher of the faith, who reserves the right to mandate the content of RE programs within the schools under his care (NCEC, 2008). Usually, RE curriculum planners in Catholic Education Offices operate under this mandate, and design the syllabus with the approval of the Diocesan Bishop.

While each diocese and archdiocese will have its own particular "flavour" and endorse its own particular approach to religious education, there is a body of content and knowledge which comes from the Tradition of the Church which needs to be taught and explored in systematic way. Such a notion derives from several Church documents, including *The General Directory for Catechesis* (1997), which states that religious education in schools "appear as a scholastic discipline with the same systematic demands and the same rigor as other disciplines" (# 73).

SOURCE DOCUMENT

The General Directory for Catechesis (1997)

> … religious instruction in schools appear as a scholastic discipline with the same systematic demands and the same rigor as other disciplines. It must present the Christian message with the same seriousness and the same depth which other disciplines present their knowledge … it should engage in a necessary interdisciplinary dialogue … religious instruction in schools underpins, activates, develops and completes the educational activity of the school.
>
> GDC (1997, # 73)

ACTIVITY 7.1

> In your own words, discuss with a partner the essence of the above excerpt from the General Directory for Catechesis (1997).

In other words, religious education is a discipline in its own right. It contains its own content – a body of knowledge, skills and understandings. It should be taught with the same academic rigor as other subjects in the curriculum. So, from where then does the content for religious education come?

Catechism of the Catholic Church

In recent years, the body of content which forms the basis of various RE syllabi, curriculum guidelines and textual materials has been guided by the *Catechism of the Catholic Church* (1994). In this document, the content is organized around *The Four Pillars of Faith*:

- The Profession of Faith (Creed)
- The Celebration of the Christian Mystery (Sacraments)
- Life in Christ (Christian morality)
- Christian Prayer (Prayer)

ACTIVITY 7.2

> Locate a copy of the Catechism of the Catholic Church and look through the contents pages. Locate each of the Four Pillars (they are major headings). What kind of content is listed under each of the Pillars?

An initial delineation of the content headings, or themes, contained in each of the Four Pillars of Faith is set out below.

The Profession of Faith (Creed)
God, Revelation, Scripture, creedal beliefs, beliefs about human life and the world, Jesus Christ, the Holy Spirit, the Church, Mary, the saints, the forgiveness of sins, everlasting life.
The Celebration of the Christian Mystery (Sacraments)
The Liturgy, each of the seven Sacraments, other Liturgical celebrations
Life in Christ (Christian Morality)
The dignity of the human person, the ten commandments, Christian Testament moral teachings, the development of conscience, personal and social sin, the demands of social justice, Catholic social teaching, grace and Christian holiness
Christian Prayer (Prayer)
Traditional and contemporary prayer, the Psalms, the Our Father, newer forms of prayer, Marian prayer, meditation, prayer in the Gospels

The content contained in *the Catechism of the Catholic Church* is not intended for use with students in Catholic schools in the form in which it appears in this document. Clearly, the presentation of content in *the Catechism of the Catholic Church* is complex, and the intended audience is in fact the bishops and clergy of the dioceses. It becomes the role of the curriculum planners, working with the approval of the diocesan bishop or archbishop, to translate this content into units of work which are appropriate for both teachers and students in Catholic schools. Each diocese will have its own particular way of translating and arranging this material for use with students, and its own approaches for delivering and enabling students to engage with this material.

ACTIVITY 7.3

> Compare and contrast two sets of diocesan syllabi or guidelines produced in different dioceses during the last five years. How is the teaching of material organized? What approach is endorsed?

Following are some broad examples of how the religious education syllabus, or elements of it, has been organized at the diocesan level. The purpose is not to explore the particular approach of each diocese, but rather to briefly explore how the content has been arranged, and whether or not it reflects the Four Pillars as outlined in *The Catechism of the Catholic Church*.

Example 1: Religious Education in the Archdiocese of Melbourne

Below is the initial section of a curriculum schema, developed by the Catholic Education Office Melbourne which indicates, at broad levels, how the content of religious education in the Archdiocese of Melbourne is organized. The section is from the *Coming to Know, Worship and Love* (2008) curriculum framework. Note that the content has been divided into "strands". It is intended that each of the five strands will be addressed through the religious education curriculum in each Year Level of the Catholic primary school. Notice how the strands reflect The Four Pillars of *The Catechism of the Catholic Church*.

> In the discipline of religious education students form religious knowledge and understandings and ways of thinking and responding through the exploration of five specific areas of church life, teaching and practice. Named as content strands, these five areas emerge from an understanding of the Church and its life where the person of Jesus is central. These content strands are drawn from the goals. They are:
>
> 1. Scripture and Jesus
>
> 2. Church and Community
>
> 3. God, Religion and Life
>
> 4. Prayer, Liturgy and Sacraments
>
> 5. Morality and Justice
>
> In order for students to form deep understandings of key church beliefs and practices in the context of everyday life it is necessary to integrate the content strands in one unit or topic…In this way students make links between these significant areas of church life and teaching and use these to construct meaning around their relationship to God, self, others and their world.

Coming To Know Worship and Love (2008, p. 16)

Developing this into a workable, sequential curriculum is more challenging. Below are two lists of *exemplar units* from the *Coming to Know, Worship and Love* (2008) curriculum framework. In this curriculum there are two components – a student text, and a curriculum framework. The curriculum framework was devised to support the text based religious education approach directed for use in Catholic schools in the Archdiocese of Melbourne. The *exemplar units* below indicate how the content might be organized in the Senior Primary years (Grades 5 and 6, students aged between about 10 and 12). In this adaptation, reference is also made to the relevant chapters from the *To Know, Worship and Love (KWL)* student texts which support each unit. Notice how the material has been divided into *Units of Work* (*Exemplar Units* as they are termed in this document) which reflect one or more of the stands around which the content has been organized. Notice also how many of the general themes indicated under each of the Four Pillars of Faith (Catechism of the Catholic Church) are reflected in these units of work.

Exemplar units of work: Level 4, Grade 5

Life Is Good (KWL, Year 5: Chapter 1, God the Creator; Chapter 17, Respect for Life)

A Time of God's Generosity (KWL, Year 5: Chapter 3, Lent;, Chapter 6, Holy Week)

New Beginnings (KWK, Year 5: Chapter 7, He Is Risen!)

The Gifts and Fruits of the Spirit (KWL, Year 5: Chapter 8, The Spirit is Alive; Chapter 9, The Holy Trinity)

The Seven Sacraments: Signs of God's Presence (KWL, Year 5: Chapter 4, The Seven Sacraments; Chapter 5, Reconciliation and Healing; Chapter 13, The Sacrament of Holy Orders; Chapter 14, We Receive Jesus in the Eucharist; Chapter 15, We Worship Jesus in the Eucharist)

Mission Impossible (KWL, Year 5: Chapter 2, Virtues; Chapter 10, A Heart to Love; Chapter 11: Our Church Community)

People of God in Australia (KWL, Year 5: Chapter 11, Our Church Community; Chapter 12, Our Church in Australia: How it Began)

Waiting for the Messiah (KWL, Year 5: Chapter 18, Mary Our Mother; Chapter 19: We Celebrate Advent and Christmas)

***Adapted* Coming to Know, Worship and Love (2008)**

> *Exemplar units of work: Level 4, Grade 6*
>
> **Teach Us To Pray!** (KWL, Year 6: Chapter 9, Teach Us To Pray)
>
> **Lent to Easter: We Are Transformed!** (KWL, Year 6: Chapter 3, Freedom to Choose; Chapter 4, Reconciliation; Chapter 5, Journeying from Lent to Holy Week; Chapter 6, Resurrection and Ascension)
>
> **My Mission in the Faith Community!** (KWL, Year 6: Chapter 1, One in Christ Jesus; Chapter 8, The Church, People of Pentecost; Chapter 11, One in the Spirit)
>
> **A Community of Faith – Called to Serve!** (KWL, Year 6: Chapter 2, Blessed Are You!; Chapter 7, One, Holy, Catholic and Apostolic; Chapter 14, Mary, the Faithful Disciple)
>
> **The Mass: Sacrifice and Meal** (KWL, Year 6: Chapter 12, We Gather to Worship)
>
> **Sacred Stories – Sacred Peoples** (KWL, Year 6: Chapter 10, The Word of God; Chapter 13, The God We Worship)
>
> **Be Compassionate, Choose Justice!** (KWL, Year 6: Chapter 1, One in Christ Jesus; Chapter 2, Blessed Are You; Chapter 17, Our Christian Mission)
>
> **Wait For The Saviour – He Will Come!** (KWL, Year 6: Chapter 10, The Word of God; Chapter 19, Advent People)

Adapted Coming to Know, Worship and Love (2008)

ACTIVITY 7.4

> Using copies of the To Know, Worship and Love student text and the Coming To Know, Worship and Love curriculum framework, align the exemplar units from the framework with the chapters from the student text as indicated in the table above. To what extent do the exemplar units listed above and the corresponding chapters from the To Know, Worship and Love student texts cover each of The Four Pillars as outline in the Catechism of the Catholic Church?

Example 2: Religious Education in the Archdiocese of Hobart

Below is part of the doctrinal schema proved by the Archdiocese of Hobart for its religious education syllabus document *Good News for Living* (Level 3, Grades 3 and 4).

- We are all created in God's image.
- The Scriptures contain many stories and images that give us some insights into the mystery of God.
- God trusts and forgives us.
- God calls us to reach out in love to each other.
- We are gifted and graced, able to share in the transforming love of God.
- The father of Jesus is our father too.
- The Holy Spirit enables us to live in communication with God and other people.

ACTIVITY 7.5

Find the points listed above on the Hobart Catholic Education Office website. Each point is cross-referenced with the Catechism of the Catholic Church. Match up each point with a Catechism reference and describe the link between the two.

Example 3: Religious Education in English-Speaking Canada

The table below lists the scope and sequence for the Grade 3 curriculum in the *Born in the Spirit* English Canadian catechetical series.

Scope and Sequence Year 3		
Unit 1 *We welcome and gather in the Spirit* Welcoming Dreaming with God Let's celebrate	**Unit 2** *The Holy Spirit gathers and feds us at Eucharist* The Holy Spirit is at work among us The Holy Spirit is at work in the Eucharist We celebrate Eucharist	**Unit 3** *The Holy Spirit calls and anoints us in Baptism and Conformation* We belong to the Sunday assembly We come together signed with God's spirit We are called into service by the Spirit
Unit 4 *The Holy Spirit comes upon Advent people* In the Spirit we wait for God's coming In the Spirit we wait for Mary The Spirit is upon us as Advent	**Unit 5** *The Holy Spirit dwells in Jesus* God dwells in us The Holy Spirit fills Jesus with God's power The Holy Spirit works in Jesus	**Unit 6** *The Holy Spirit dwells in the followers of Jesus* Jesus shares his mission with the disciples The spirit is upon us We meet people of the Spirit
Unit 7 *The Holy Spirit fills the whole earth* You stretch out the heavens like a tent Crowned with God's glory The earth shall yield its truths	**Unit 8** *The Holy Spirit reconciles people* Jesus brings the spirit of forgiveness In the power of the Spirit we forgive In the death of Jesus we are reconciled	**Unit 9** *The Holy Spirit gives new life* Alleluia He is risen The Holy Spirit renews the face of the earth We have new life in the Spirit
Unit 10 *The Holy Spirit is alive* We are the Church spirit filled we reach out to serve We celebrate that we are the Church		

ACTIVITY 7.6

> What is your analysis of the content overview given above? Is it comprehensive? Are there any areas that are not included and should be? Are any areas over represented?

Example 4: Religious Education in the Archdiocese of Brisbane

Ten key principles guide the design and development of the religion curriculum in the Archdiocese of Brisbane. They are:

- The classroom teaching and learning of Religion should reflect the philosophy, content focus, structure, academic rigor and assessment and reporting modes used in other curriculum areas.
- The content should reflect a Catholic Christian worldview that integrates faith, life and culture.
- The design and development needs to build on the best practice in Religious Education currently being enacted in the schools and colleges of the Archdiocese and the broader educational community.
- The design and development should continue to align with a reconceptualist approach to Religious Education (learning about religion and learning from and through religion).
- The framework should bring into closer alignment the two dimensions of Religious Education – classroom teaching of religion and the religious life of the school.
- The pedagogical direction should reflect an inquiry-based approach to learning that aligns closely with current developments in the Australian Curriculum.
- The aim of Religious Education should be adjusted to better reflect the reality of most schools.
- Core content needs to be presented in a clear, precise way, written in plain English and expressed using educational rather than exclusively theological language.
- Where possible, content should embrace an ecumenical perspective and reflect the multi-faith context and reality of contemporary religion classrooms.
- The structure and presentation of material should resemble the Australian Curriculum and build on the *Melbourne Declaration on Educational Goals for Young Australians*.

Content for the classroom teaching and learning of Religion is organised around four strands with three sub-strands for each. These reflect the changing needs of the contemporary Religion classroom. The new strands and sub-strands are presented as follows:

Strand	Sub-strand
Sacred Texts	Old Testament; New Testament; Spiritual Writings and Wisdom
Beliefs	God, Jesus, Spirit; Human Existence; Religions of the World
Church	Liturgy and Sacraments; Communion and Community; Church History
Christian Life	Moral Formation; Mission and Service; Prayer and Spirituality

A key feature of this document is that it attempts to address the multicultural and multi-faith dimensions by including in the "Beliefs" strand a study of Religions of the World at both primary/elementary and secondary/junior high/high school levels.

ACTIVITY 7.7

> What is your reaction to the ten key principles that guide the design and development of the religion curriculum in the Archdiocese of Brisbane? Are there any areas missing in the Strands and Sub-strands?

Some Common Characteristics

As can be seen from the examples above, the religious education syllabus in each of the dioceses reflects the broad areas as indicated by the Four Pillars of Faith in *The Catechism of the Catholic Church*. It is pertinent to note also that in addition to the Four Pillars of Faith, as foundational as these are, religious education is also informed by various other sources. These include (but are not limited to):

- Other Church documents (e.g., *The Religious Dimension of Education in a Catholic School*)
- Various Church teachings related to methodology
- Diocesan policies and priorities
- Government policies and initiatives
- National and State development in curriculum design and pedagogy (e.g., assessment and reporting)
- Educational research, including research related to religious education and culture.

While these sources have some impact upon the content of religious education, they certainly influence the design of the religious education curricula as a whole. They may also influence how the content of the religious education curriculum is taught at the classroom level. This is particularly so in relation to educational research and curriculum design and pedagogy generally.

Conclusion

Ultimately it is the Archbishop, or diocesan Bishop, in his role as the principal teacher of the faith, who reserves the right to mandate the content of religious education programs within the schools under his care (NCEC, 2008). Usually, RE curriculum planners in Catholic Education Offices operate under this mandate, and design the curriculum with the approval of the Diocesan Bishop. These planners take into account not only the content to be covered, but also other pertinent factors which influence the design of the curriculum generally.

Although each diocese has its own particular methodology, and its own particular way of organizing material, the examples presented in this chapter indicate that the content covered is similar. Irrespective of the organization of material, you will notice that each of the examples presented reflects the key principle stated in the *General Directory for Catechesis* and also in *The Religious Dimension of Education in a Catholic School*, that religious education is a scholastic discipline. It should therefore be approached with the same systematic demands and the same rigor as other academic subjects in the curriculum.

In addition, the selection and positioning of the content of religious education is also influenced and informed by other policies and initiatives, particularly national and state developments in curriculum design. It is also influenced by the wealth of contemporary education research, especially research related to religious education and western culture generally.

Brisbane Catholic Education. (2012). *The new religion curriculum, Archdiocese of Brisbane*. Accessed http://recurriculum.weebly.com/about-the-curriculum.html

Catholic Diocese of Ballarat. (2005). *Awakenings: Core document religious education P-12 curriculum*. Ballarat: Catholic Diocese of Ballarat.

Catholic Education Office, Melbourne. (2008). *Coming to know, worship and love: A religious education curriculum framework for Catholic schools in the Archdiocese of Melbourne*. Melbourne: Catholic Education Office.

Catholic Education Office, Archdiocese of Hobart. (2005). *Good news for living: A curriculum framework for religious education in the Archdiocese of Hobart*. Hobart: Catholic Education Office.

Congregation for Catholic Education. (1998). *Religious dimension of education in a Catholic school: Guidelines for reflection and renewal*. Homebush, NSW: St. Paul's Publications.

Congregation for the Clergy. (1997). *General directory for catechesis*. Homebush, NSW: St. Paul's Publications.

Elliott, P. (Gen Ed.). (2003). *To know, worship and love* student text series. Melbourne: James Goold House Publications.

National Catholic Education Commission. (2008). *Religious education in dialogue: Curriculum around Australia*. Canberra, ACT: National Catholic Education Commission.

The Holy See. (1994). *The catechism of the Catholic church*. Homebush, NSW: St. Paul's Publications.

CHAPTER 8

From Objectives to Outcomes to Lesson Plans

ACTIVITY 8.1

> Imagine that you were trying to explain to someone who had never taught RE before what you can achieve in a typical lesson. Be as specific as you can, it may help to think about a particular lesson that you have taught or would like to teach.

Typically there is much that a good RE teacher wants to achieve in a lesson. Usually it is helpful to distinguish between goals for one lesson as opposed to a number of lessons. Also many of the goals have different foci. Thinking about what is to be achieved, and stating these goals in clear precise language, can greatly assist teachers working within a contemporary educational approach to religious education.

In the *Ontario Catholic elementary curriculum policy document* in religious education the idea of what is to be achieved over a period of time are called overall expectations. In the Grade 1 Believing Strand students are expected to, amongst other things:

- Demonstrate an understanding of the Bible as the inspired story of the Revelation of God

- Demonstrate an understanding of the Church as the people who are formed into a believing community

- Demonstrate how in the scriptures, the people came to know God

To assist in moving from broad expectations to manageable plans it is useful to distinguish between objectives and outcomes. Objectives are reached over a period of time – they can be thought of as relatively long-term goals. They usually do not relate to a specific lesson and contain a number of different elements.

Below are a number of objectives taken from the *Guidelines for Religious Education of Students in the Archdiocese of Melbourne (1995)*:

- Explore and appreciate some of the religious art forms of Christian cultural groups

- Grow in apperception of the prayers and traditions in the Church that have been passed on from generation to generation

- Reflect on their experiences of disappointment and failure, and appreciate that they can reach out to Jesus at such times

ACTIVITY 8.2

> Imagine that you are asked to design a number of lessons that set out to meet one of the objectives above. How would you structure teaching and learning activities that meet this objective?

Take a closer look at the first objective listed above. It contains two verbs, explore and appreciate. Each word has a different connotation. If you are asked to explore something this implies that your task is to seek out and investigate new things. Appreciate is a more difficult concept for it implies that you already know something about the topic, have explored it to some extent, and are now in a position to develop a sense of the importance and significance of what you have been exposed to.

Now ask yourself how you would you help students at, say, middle primary level, to explore religious art forms. To achieve this you could use teaching and learning activities such as:

- Showing students images of Christian religious art from around the world
- Explain in more detail specific pieces of art
- Give students a number of examples of art and ask them to name similarities and differences
- Ask students to bring in or describe religious art from their own homes
- Read a document which explains some of the features of Christian art
- Designing students own Christian art in a particular style
- Focus on one region of the world and look at the Christian art that is produced there
- Complete a worksheet that sets out the history of Christian art

This is not an exhaustive list but gives a clear indication on how the teacher can incorporate a number of teaching and learning strategies that help students explore a particular topic. Once a number of these specific goals have been stated there is allowance for other questions about the students' learning to be asked. One such question relates to whether each goal has been achieved. This is an important aspect of classroom learning. Usually teachers incorporate assessment tasks into their planing as a way of monitoring student learning. Each of the activities listed above could be matched to some type of assessment task. Take the first task listed above; this could be tied to an assessment task such as asking students to identify correctly where certain Christian art forms originated. Notice that all of the activities that are listed above relate in some way to the cognitive learning of students. Students are asked to read, describe, complete worksheets and design pieces of art in a particular way. Another term for this type of statement is **cognitive outcome**. A cognitive outcome is a brief statement that sets out the knowledge and skills that students are intended to achieve by the end of a specified period – usually one lesson.

Table 8.1: Some features of cognitive outcomes

Are specific
Are usually easily measured
Focused on growth in knowledge
Often connected to assessments
Main focus of classroom religious education
Numerous – a typical lesson contains many cognitive outcomes

A good way to frame cognitive outcomes is to think in terms of the type of verb used. This describes the main action of the outcome. Note that there are levels of complexity of verbs. Some, such as *name* and *list*, describe simple and straightforward tasks. Others, such as *critiquing* and *reconceptualize* involve elaborate processes. Below is a table comprising of verbs taken from Bloom's taxonomy of cognitive process. This table is divided up into six categories: remembering, understanding, applying, analysing, evaluating and creating.

Table 8.2: Some processes involved in cognitive outcomes

Remembering
Recognizing; Recalling; Retrieving knowledge from memory; Identifying; Naming.
Understanding
Interpreting; Exemplifying: Finding a specific example or illustration of a concept or principle; Classifying; Summarising; Comparing; Explaining; Paraphrasing; Translating; Representing; Clarifying; Illustrating; Categorizing; Abstracting; Commenting; Generalising; Extrapolating; Interpolating; Predicting; Concluding; Contrasting; Matching; Constructing models
Applying
Executing; Implementing; Carrying out; Using.
Analysing
Differentiating; Distinguishing; Organizing; Selecting; Focusing; Outlining; Structuring; Integrating.
Evaluating
Checking; Critiquing; Detecting; Testing; Coordinating; Judging.
Creating
Generating; Planning; Producing; Hypothesising; Designing; Constructing.

ACTIVITY 8.3

Use some of the terms listed in the table above to create cognitive outcomes, such as, by the end of this lesson students will:

- Contrast two interpretations of Matthew 28: 16-20

- Plan a nativity role play
- Recognize the main features of a church

From Activity to Outcome

In a primary or elementary school RE lesson scripture is often used in a variety of ways. Often a passage is read in order to give context to a future activity. Below is a passage from scripture, Luke 24: 36-43.

> He himself stood among them, and said to them, *Peace be with you*! In a state of alarm and fright, they thought that they were seeing a ghost. But he said, *Why are you so agitated, and why are there doubts rising in your hearts? Look at my hands and my feet; yes, it is I indeed. Touch me, and see for yourselves; a ghost has no flesh and bones as you can see I have.* And as he said this he showed them his hands and his feet. Their joy was so great that they could not believe it, and they stood there dumbfounded; so he said to them, *Have you anything here to eat?* And they offered him a piece of grilled fish, which he took and ate before their eyes.

In the case of the reading from scripture above, teachers can frame a cognitive outcome using a poor descriptive verb such as *understand – by the end of the lesson students will understand Luke 24: 36-43*. The difficulty with using a verb like this is that it is not clear what skills and knowledge students should acquire and how the teacher is gong to help students achieve this. Contrast the use of the verb, *understand*, with some of the outcomes listed below:

By the end of this lesson students will be able to:

- list words like: dumbfounded, agitated, flesh, as well as any other words that they do not understand
- examine a dictionary and written down the meaning of these words
- discuss with others how they would have felt if they had seen someone who they thought had died
- plan a response to what they would have said to Jesus in these circumstances
- name what Jesus ate and explained the significance of this action
- comment on Jesus' behaviour in the story
- contrast the attitude of Jesus and the disciples
- create a dialogue between two disciples on what they learned after their experience of seeing Jesus again
- compare this story with others from scripture that they have read

Listed above are a number of cognitive outcomes which all seek to amplify the instruction to understand. To state your task as to help students understand something, without qualification, does not lead into an obvious series of teaching and learning strategies. Properly framed cognitive outcomes, by contrast, are closely linked with what teachers do in the classroom and lend themselves, almost naturally, to evaluation.

Affective Outcomes

My students know all about this topic – they can describe, list, categorise, comment, construct and lots of other things. It's still really important to me that they grow as people and are not just developing into loud know-alls.

- Comment on this statement

The teacher above has expressed a comment that touches the heart of the teaching profession. Most teachers would like to see their students grow up to be well-rounded individuals and not merely be crammed with information. To this end it is important that teachers pay attention to some of the affective goals of teaching. It is important to recognise, however, that there is no conflict between cognitive and affective goals. In fact, they work in harmony. One good way to achieve affective outcomes is to teach to well-thought-out, achievable and precise cognitive outcomes. Many of the cognitive outcomes described earlier pertain to higher order thinking – they are not just concerned with relatively simple tasks such as remembering pieces of information. In framing cognitive goals there is great scope to reward creative processes, and if taught well these meet many of the developmental goals that are often the subject of affective outcomes.

Affective outcomes address some of the larger issues that teachers seek to incorporate in their teaching but which do not sit easily with specific cognitive outcomes. The first objective discussed earlier, *explore and appreciate some of the religious art forms of Christian cultural groups,* uses the verb *appreciate*. If we are asked to appreciate something one of the first things that we notice as educators is that this is a much more elusive concept than to explore something. A student may be very familiar with a topic, seem to know a lot about it, but do we know if she appreciates it? There is no easy answer to this question. The point that is being made here is that some of the teaching that we do in RE time is directed to goals which, whilst important, have a different character to cognitive outcomes. A collective title for these is *affective outcomes*. Affective outcomes are usually used to describe the goals of an entire unit or program. They are usually stated in terms of desired or hoped for results, such as, by *the end of the Unit is it hoped that students will.*

Table 3: Some features of affective outcomes

Are broad
Are usually difficult to measure
Are focused on development of attitudes, values, emotions and faith responses
Are expressed as desirable outcomes, as in something to be hoped for or offered
Can be associated with the whole school ethos
Are not as numerous as cognitive outcomes

Affective outcomes describe a range of processes by using a series of descriptive verbs. Some of the verbs and terms commonly used as part of affective outcomes are given below:

- reflect
- appreciate
- be sensitive to
- respond
- show respect
- sympathise
- express solidarity with
- accept
- be responsible
- participate
- offer

Listed below are some affective outcomes that relate to a variety of topics in religious education – each relate to a whole unit of work, rather than to a specific lesson:

- Students will be offered the opportunity to reflect on their lives in light of reading John 15: 12-13
- It is hoped that students gain a greater insight into the suffering of the Jewish people
- It is hoped that students grow in appreciation of the importance of St Paul for Christians
- Students will be given a chance to express their thoughts on this topic through prayer
- Students will be offered time to reflect on their stories
- Students may creatively respond to class initiatives

ACTIVITY 8.4

> Imagine that you were teaching a unit on the Kingdom of God. This incorporates the scripture reading given earlier, Luke 24: 36-43. Try to state some affective outcomes that would be appropriate in such a unit. State your outcomes in the form: By the end of this unit it is hoped that.

A reading such as the one from Luke 24: 36-43 could be used for a unit that incorporated the following affective outcomes.

It is hoped that by the end of the unit students:

- develop an appreciation for the impact that the resurrection of Jesus had on the first Christians
- realise that they have a place in the Kingdom of God
- develop an awareness of the importance of the risen Lord for themselves and for all Christians
- will participate in a liturgy that celebrates Jesus' presence amongst us.

A Word on Spiritual Outcomes

A third type of outcome that is used in religious education is spiritual outcomes. These usually call for some type of faithful response from students. They are framed in terms of an invitation to respond. A good way to understand spiritual outcomes is to compare them with cognitive and affective outcomes.

Take a topic such as Advent. This is a theme that is tackled at many levels in the primary school. Below are some cognitive outcomes that could be used in a unit on Advent or as part of teaching about the liturgical year.

At the end of the lesson students will have:

- Identify the Christmas tree as one of the symbols of Advent
- Described Advent as part of the liturgical year
- Compared the story of the birth of Jesus from the Gospels of Matthew and Luke
- Designed a series of textboxes that tell the story of the birth of Jesus

We can frame affective outcomes for the same lesson, bearing in mind that affective outcomes usually relate to units rather than lessons.

By the end of the unit:

- Students will be given the opportunity to participate in an Advent liturgy
- It is hoped that students will appreciate the importance of Advent to Christians and have reflected on the importance of Advent for them

A spiritual outcome involves a direct invitation for growth or participation from the individual. It often makes reference to the Christian tradition or the way that God acts in the life of the individual. Like affective outcomes, spiritual outcomes usually relate to a unit. A suitable spiritual outcome for the Advent unit could be:

- Students are invited to consider how the message of Advent could challenge and change the way they deal with others, especially the lowly and outcast.

An Example of Cognitive, Affective and Spiritual Outcomes

Below is an extract from the *To Know, Worship and Love* student text, Level 3:

> At the Last Supper the Lord Jesus promised that when he left his disciples he would send them the Holy Spirit (John 16:7-8). After Jesus ascended to heaven, Mary and the disciples waited for the Holy Spirit. Ten days later, on Pentecost Sunday, a mighty wind shook the house and they saw what looked like "tongues of fire" over their heads. They were able to praise God and speak in languages they had never learned before. The Holy Spirit had come and changed their lives! The disciples knew that the Holy Spirit was with them and now they were able to spread the Good News of Jesus. Many people joined them as followers of Jesus. The promise of Jesus had come true.
>
> The Church remembers and celebrates the coming of the Holy Spirit at Pentecost. Above all, we celebrate and receive the Holy Spirit through the seven Sacraments. All Sacraments give us grace, the life and love of God. In each sacrament the Spirit works in a different way, to guide and strengthen us to live as Jesus' followers.

ACTIVITY 8.5

> Imagine that you were using the extract above in a lesson. Write down as many cognitive outcomes as you can that relate to this extract. Then try to write some affective and spiritual outcomes that could also be used with this activity.

When developing cognitive outcomes a good starting point is to think in terms of the activities that you will use in the lesson. From these then develop cognitive outcomes. If the extract above was being used the following outcomes, as well as many others, could be used.

By the end of the lesson students will have:

- Listed the words in bold type into their glossaries
- Discussed the meaning of the words amongst themselves and checked these meanings with the teacher
- Recalled those present at the first Pentecost
- Created a flowchart which shows the main events of the first Pentecost Sunday
- Explored the impact of the coming of the Holy Spirit by planning a short role-play

Following on from the cognitive outcomes of the lesson affective outcomes can also be developed. For example, by the end of this unit students will have:

- Developed an appreciation of the importance of Pentecost for Christians
- Respected the views of others by listening to their opinions
- Gained some understanding of the role of the Holy Spirit in the Church

Finally a spiritual outcome, that invites a faith response from students, can be used. For example, by the end of this unit students:

- Will be invited to see how the coming of the Holy Spirit can transform their lives and help them spread the message of Jesus.

ACTIVITY 8.6

> We began this chapter considering how we can move from objectives to outcomes. In the Pentecost activity just described a number of outcomes were listed: cognitive, affective and spiritual. Now work backwards and try to list an objective that all these outcomes are trying to meet. Remember objectives relate, at least, to a whole unit and are made up of cognitive, affective and spiritual aspects.

Using Outcomes to Plan a Lesson

One of the most useful things about using outcomes is that they assist teachers to plan lessons in religious education. The planning process can be divided into a number of tasks

1. Identify the topic that you wish to cover

This is a straightforward task and one that is tied into the curriculum framework that you are following. This will also confirm what grade level the lesson is designed for and give some idea on assumptions about students in the planning document. The key here is to be aware of what is to be covered in one lesson, knowing that in a unit of work there are a series of lessons in sequence (planning a unit of work is be covered in another chapter of this text).

2. Nominate which outcomes you wish to cover in one lesson

In planning a lesson most teachers start with outcomes and then move to activities, but it is possible to reveres this order depending on individual preference.

Outcomes are well suited to focussing on teaching and learning in a particular lesson. Often when considering a lesson in religious education there is a tendency to think about more abstract objectives. This is often a necessary first step but in a lesson plan the key task is to distil down into a certain amount of time an aspect of a much wider learning framework.

Take, for instance, a unit on scripture. The objective here could be to help students demonstrate an understanding of the Bible as the inspired story of the Revelation of God. This is a broad goal and to bring it about requires, to say the least, many individual lessons. So in planning one lesson teachers need to have a sharp focus on what can be achieved in that lesson. And this is where outcomes plan a critical role.

For the objective mentioned many cognitive outcomes could be used to give the lesson a strong sense of purpose and direction.

- Nominate some cognitive outcomes that meet fit the above mentioned objective.

3. Plan activities for the lesson

Based on your topic and how long the lesson is, start to think about what activities will form the basis of your lesson. In planning one lesson it is not necessary to cover a wide range of pedagogical techniques. The key is to identify some teaching and learning strategies that fit best with the outcomes that you wish to cover in the lesson. Many teachers find it easier to break up the lesson into parts and plan different strategies for each section.

One common way of dividing up a lesson is to look at it in three major sections; introductory activities, main body and concluding activities. This breakdown can be useful, especially when it comes to allocation time for each activity. Time estimates are important for they give a good indication on what the main task of the lesson will be. They are not, however, inflexible and are designed to be a guide only.

In choosing activities for a lesson, consideration should be given to the age of the students, their background and previous learning. Recognition of different learning styles should be acknowledged and teaching and learning strategies that highlight the capacities of students should be emphasized.

Anderson, L., & Krathwohl, D. (Eds). (2001). *Taxonomy of learning, teaching and assessment: A revision of Bloom's taxonomy of educational objectives*. New York: Longman.

Sawyer, R. (2006). *The Cambridge handbook of the learning sciences*. Cambridge: Cambridge University Press.

Websites

The Carnegie Foundation for the Advancement of Teaching
http://carnegiefoundation.org/home.htm

The Active Learning Site
http//active-learning.com/index.html

The IDEA Center at Kansas State U
http://ksu.edu/

CHAPTER 9

Planning a Unit of Work in Religious Education

A Unit of Work is a sequence of lessons and covers a number of weeks of the school year. A Unit of Work enables the teacher to think in terms of a broader range of topics and to develop teaching and learning strategies along graded and sequential lines. This more diffuse focus is educationally relevant because good teaching requires a consistent effort over a period of time and this is difficult to do if a teacher is concentrating on a series of one-off lessons.

ACTIVITY 9.1

> Let's Find Some Units! There are many examples of completed units of work in religious education. Spend some time looking at these either in hard copy or online. Identify some that you think are high quality, bring them to class and share them with others.
>
> - List 3 key features that you like about the unit.
>
> If you are having trouble getting started here is a site of RE units from the Edmonton Catholic School Board, Edmonton, Alberta Canada. http://education.alberta.ca/parents/resources/handbook.aspx

Locating the Unit

ACTIVITY 9.2

> Imagine that you are teaching a topic with which you have some familiarity – the subject matter is not important.
>
> - How, in general terms, would you teach this to 6 year olds as opposed to 11 year olds?
> - List some of the teaching strategies that you think are appropriate to the younger students.
> - What assessment tasks are more suited to older students?
> - Are there any generic aspects of teaching – that is – they apply to all ages?
> - What, if any, are some of the differences you need to consider in presenting a Religious Education topic to students of different ages?

The first task in planning a Unit of Work is to locate the unit within a teaching context. The most basic questions to ask here are: how old are the students and how long will the unit be? The age of the students is easy to determine, but in planning a unit some thought should be given to how the age of the learner impacts on the way the unit is developed. Before planning a unit at a particular grade level, RE teachers should ask how they would approach the same topic if the students were older or younger. This practice develops in the teacher the habit of seeing students as a differentiated body and not some generic mass. Take, for example, a typical RE unit dealing with sacraments. In planning a unit on this theme at Grade 1 level, consider how it would it be taught at, say, Grade 6 level. To answer this question in detail would require a comparison of at least two Units of Work, and this is not the task here. Consideration of Units of Work across the curriculum, nonetheless, gives the RE teacher a sense of the developmental character of the discipline and can generate useful questions about the specific needs of learners at particular age levels. It is also helpful to have an idea of where the curriculum and the learner are headed in terms of what is expected of them in later years.

Some Preliminary Considerations

1. Ascertaining prior learning

ACTIVITY 9.3

> Discuss the statement: My students know nothing about this topic – I have to start from scratch!
>
> 1. What implications does this view have for planning a Unit of Work?

It is important in planning a unit to ascertain prior leanings. This can be done formally by consulting the curriculum of the school to see what the students have done in previous years. Asking other teachers is another way of gaining valuable information about prior learning. This is especially important if you are doing a topic that has already been done in the earlier year levels. It is not unusual for important themes to be repeated in the curriculum. If this is the case be familiar with what teaching and learning activities have already been used and also be aware of attempting to pre-set the Unit in a more detailed and sophisticated way than previously.

2. Determining what is already available

Many schools have excellent material that can be used to great effect in religious education. One of the most useful activities an RE teacher can do prior to developing a unit is a careful audit of the library or RE resource area. This can be especially useful for items such as audiovisual teaching aides. Searching in this way can take time but it is a very useful investment, especially when you come to brainstorm activities for your Unit.

3. How long should a unit be?

One of the great advantages in planning Units of Work is that it allows for the development of large *chunks* of material. How long the units should be depends on the local condition of the school and demands of external educational agencies. A good working definition of a Unit of Work is that it should run from between 10 to 15 lessons or contact periods. This assumes lesson lengths of about 50 minutes. This is a significant amount of teaching time without being too long and difficult to plan for.

The unit of work as a detailed instruction to a fellow professional

One way of describing a Unit of Work is that it aims to be something that, when given to another RE teacher, should provide him or her with all they need to teach the sequence of lessons provided. This is somewhat analogous to what scientists try to do when they prepare an experimental report. Another scientist who reads this should be able to replicate the experiment successfully. A good Unit of Work should be able, without much further explanation, to be used by another RE teacher. It should contain enough instructions, activities, explanatory notes and additional exercises to be useful. The core activities should be highlighted and superfluous information relegated to the appendices. Just as trying to duplicate an experiment can be marred by too much detail, the efficacy of a Unit of Work in RE can be hindered by a lack of focus or presenting too much material that has not been properly analysed or edited.

Preliminary stages

1. Consult the school's RE curriculum. Be sure of what precedes and follows the unit. If the curriculum is insufficiently developed, at least be clear in your own mind about what precedes and follows this unit in your RE class.

2. Discuss your unit with the REC and other experienced RE teachers.

3. Examine whether there are textbooks, Guidelines or other curriculum documents that are relevant to the topic you are teaching. Read them carefully and let them inform what you are planning.

4. Do some background reading or other research on the topic you wish to cover. This is an important step, especially if you are venturing into unfamiliar territory. Utilise the fact that if you do not know a lot about a particular area you can usually place yourself on a very steep learning curve by doing only a comparatively small amount of background research.

5. Consider the question; why am I teaching this unit? In the process of planning the answer to this question should become clearer.

Developing the plan part 1: The rough draft

1. Quickly sketch out how you think the lessons in the Unit will go. It is important from the very outset of planning a Unit of Work in RE to envisage it as a sequence of lessons and not a collection of individual lesson plans. Try and include one cognitive outcome and one teaching activity for each lesson. At this stage it is often helpful to think in terms of what you will actually do in the lesson and then to frame a cognitive outcome which meets this outcome. A rough draft will help you quickly identify those areas that are crucial and those which need further development. Write out this outline in table form. A table, which uses the example of a unit on the Eucharist aimed at middle primary, is given below.

Lesson 1	Lesson 2	Lesson 3	Final Lesson
One key outcome – eg students recall Eucharistic celebrations that they have been a part of. One key activity – students share their experiences.	Outcome – be able to describe the parts of the Mass. Activity – students complete a worksheet on the structure of the Mass.	Outcome – identify the significance of the Mass for Catholics. Activity – speaker from the parish explains some of the significance of the Mass.	Outcome – summarise what we know about the Mass. Activity - Complete a poster that captures what they have done in the Unit.

ACTIVITY 9.4

Attempt compiling an outline table for a unit of your choosing. Remember to identify the grade level of the students and give some thought to their prior leanings.

2. Identify a number of lessons in the unit that you consider to be pivotal and develop these; again, without going into complete detail. This stage enables you to get something on paper that gives you a reference point for a more detailed lesson plan. This is helpful in developing the unit as a plan of action and not just a conceptual framework. At this stage consult with other teachers and utilise the library or the RE resource centre of the school. This will help stimulate your thinking.

3. Give some thought at this stage to teaching and learning activities, assessment tasks and what further outcomes you which to achieve in the unit. Make preliminary lists of all of these. These are the types of things that *leap out at you* by being obviously relevant to the unit.

ACTIVITY 9.5

Choose a theme that you think is suitable for a Unit of Work. Write down as many activities as you think are appropriate for this topic.

4. Go back to the lesson plans that you developed in Step 1. Now fill these out with some of the activities, assessments and outcomes that you listed in the previous step. You are now at a stage where most lesson plans have outcomes, activities and assessment ideas included.

Developing the plan part 2: The final version

1. You are now ready to complete a final version of the unit using the four steps listed above as a preliminary template. Begin at Step 4 but now have a far greater attention to detail. This means, initially, identifying more carefully what exactly you are going to do in the lessons in the unit. Your attention here should be to generate teaching and learning strategies that *work*, that is, meet the demands of contemporary students and also the specified learning outcomes. Good teaching is largely typified by teachers using effective teaching and learning strategies. This sounds like a truism but it

needs to be said nonetheless. Inexperienced RE teachers often find it difficult, at least initially, to generate good teaching and learning strategies. One way of selecting good teaching activities is to consider assessments tasks. Which ones will be used and when will they be given in the sequence of lessons you have planned? For example, if you would like to use a cumulative work diary as part of your assessment, think about what the students will have to hand in as part of their diaries. Suppose that students are expected to complete, amongst other things, a glossary of key words and phrases. Allocate part of your unit to activities that enable students to meet this assessment task. To complete a glossary at some stage in the unit you will have to have teaching strategies in place that enable students to do this. At this stage of the planning process give some thought to where you will include activities like class prayer and liturgies; these are an important part of Unit planning in primary RE.

ACTIVITY 9.6

> Imagine that you are teaching a Year 3 unit on saints. Suggest some teaching and learning strategies that will enable students to complete a glossary of key terms by the end of a unit.

ACTIVITY 9.7

> Students are asked to conduct an interview with a companion of Mary Mackillop. What skills and knowledge will students need to do this task well? How would your classroom teaching enable students to meet this assessment task?

The link between assessments and teaching activities is one way of getting ideas about how to develop lessons in a unit. At this stage of unit preparation audit all the activities and assessments. It is helpful to list these down again, as this gives a clear indication of the teaching and learning activates and assessment tasks that you are offering. When listed a bias to one type of activity or assessment is more obvious. At the end of Step 5 you should have lesson plans that have detailed activities, including prayer and liturgies and assessments.

1. Now return to some of the outcomes you listed in Step 1. The outcomes that you initially listed now need further development; typically they may need to be made much more specific. As the lesson plans begin to take shape outcomes such as *students will understand …* transform into far more specific ones that include verbs such as *list, describe, compare, analyse* and *locate*. At this stage the number of outcomes increases. This is a consequence of greater specificity.

2. At this stage the unit should be taking definite shape. Include approximate times for each activity you have included. This may alter your lessons as timing an activity also makes you think more carefully about it and whether to add or eliminate some detail. It is better to include too much information and not finish everything that you have planned rather than be struggling to fill in time. It is important, however, to be clear about what the key activities are. These may not follow in sequence but are, in your judgement, pivotal to the success of that particular lesson. Rather than skip over these, leave out other more peripheral teaching and learning strategies. This

is especially important if the key activities are toward the end of the lesson. In your completed Unit of Work you may wish to highlight the key activities in a distinctive colour so that they stand out.

A series of timed activities from a unit on the history of the Catholic Church, focussing on the post war period, aimed at senior elementary/primary is given below.

Activity 1: Students read an account of post war migration to Australia. Students are asked to respond to the question *Where did these people come from and why did they choose to settle in Australia?*	Reading 5 minutes, response 5 minutes Total 10 minutes
Activity 2: Give students the handout on the conditions in Australia in the post war period. Questions are included as part of the handout.	Reading, answer questions and review. 15 minutes
Activity 3: Students, in small groups, discuss the experience of the migrants – what would it have been like to leave your homeland for a new county?	10 minutes
Activity 4: The lasting impact of the migrants. Visit a Church that was built to cater for the needs of post war migrants. What features of the Church make it stand out? Is it different from other Churches the students are familiar with? This visit may coincide with a talk from someone who works with migrant groups.	Half day

Note that any plan for a lesson in a Unit of Work estimates the length of time that activities will take. This is helpful for the planning process and is not intended to stifle an unexpected vein of interest. For example, in the table above, Activity 4 could take significantly less time or far more depending on how students react to it. This is difficult to predict accurately all the time. If an activity works well and students embrace it enthusiastically you should stick with this, provided that the pivotal parts of the lesson are identified and not neglected. This may mean returning to a pivotal activity in another part of the unit.

1. Now prepare the resources that you will need for the unit. How this is done depends on the type of teaching and learning strategies that you have chosen. An important general principle is to try and make all resources that you include in your unit as concise as possible. If, for example, you plan to give the students some background information from a book, prepare only the relevant part of the source document. Do not hand out to students wads of paper that are only remotely connected to your teaching plan. A similar point can be made about using other resources such as audio visual aids. A video can be a very appropriate teaching aid. It is unlikely, however, that students need to see a long section of a video. It is far better to nominate the exact section of the video that you will be watching.

2. The Unit of Work should now be almost complete. It should include outcomes for each lesson as well as a variety of teaching and learning activities and strategies. Now try to

compose some outcomes which span the whole unit. This is another way of making sure that the unit is a proper developmental sequence. In general if a unit is well integrated it is relatively easy to see the main focus of the unit and then to specify this into a number of unit outcomes. This is also a good time to review the affective outcomes of the unit. Affective outcomes fit in neatly with unit outcomes. Often the affective goals that you set in teaching RE are difficult to achieve in one or two lessons and can more appropriately be addressed as goals to be achieved over an entire Unit of Work.

3. At the end of your unit prepare some type of evaluation exercise. This helps you get used to the idea that once a unit has been taught it should be reviewed so that the strong and weak points of the unit can be identified. This in turn allows you to modify your Unit of Work accordingly. As part of the evaluative process include some questions that have a clear practical focus. This would include questions such as: *which activities worked well? which outcomes weren't I able to achieve? which resources need adjustment?*

Final evaluative checklist

As a means of ensuring that the Unit of Work has been properly planned try answering the following questions:

- Why am I teaching this unit?
- How does this unit fit into the school's curriculum?
- Is there an obvious sequence in the lessons in the unit?
- Is the unit informed by Textbooks, Guidelines and other relevant curriculum documents?
- Is there a range of different tasks that reflect different leaning styles?
- Are my outcomes clear and achievable?
- Could I hand this Unit of Work to another teacher with confidence that they will be able to teach it well?

Bansford, J., Brown, A., & Cocking R. (1999). *How people learn: Brain, mind, experience and school.* Washington, D.C: National Academy Press.

Cross, K., & Steadman, M. (1996). *Classroom research: Implementing the scholarship of teaching.* San Francisco: Jossey-Bass.

Davis B. (1993). *Tools for teaching.* San Francisco: Jossey-Bass.

Nolen, B. (2002) Developing an RE unit: Challenging and stimulating students. *Journal of Religious Education, 50* (1), 45-49

Weimer, M. (2002). *Learner-centered teaching: Five key changes to practice.* San Francisco: Jossey Bass.

CHAPTER 10

Differentiating the Curriculum: Catering for Diversity in Religious Education

A scenario

The students in Millie's Grade 5 classroom, around ten years of age, are investigating the books of the Bible. Millie has prepared a number of different activities in which the students are engaging. Some of the students are making lists which categorize the books of the Bible under different headings, such as myths, epic stories, poetry and song, and so forth. Some students are painting and covering empty breakfast cereal boxes to make each of the different books of the Bible. These will be placed on a specially made book shelf. Other students are preparing "trivial pursuit" type questions about the different books of the Bible for a board game. This will eventually be played by small groups of children in the classroom. Still other students are designing a billboard advertising the Books of the Bible, while others are preparing interview questions they would ask the authors of these books. These will be recorded using audio tape to make a radio program that will later be shared with students in other classrooms.

ACTIVITY 10.1

What do you notice about each of the activities that Millie has planned? Might each activity address a common outcome? What might that outcome be?

In any one particular classroom in the Catholic school there will be students who, although usually around the same age, will have different abilities, different strengths, and who will each have a preferred way or style of learning. For instance, not all students in a classroom will learn effectively if the teachers only ever plans activities which involve copious amounts of reading and writing. This way of learning will appeal to some students, but not to all. Many students may show a preference for learning visually, for example through art and drawing (visual learners). Others may seem to learn more effectively through movement and dance (kinesthetic learners). Others still may exhibit a preference for learning through music, or through listening and speaking (auditory learners). This means that the effective educator needs to plan a range of activities which aim to address the particular ways in which the students in the class may effectively learn, and enable them to demonstrate what they have learned. This process is known as ***differentiating*** the curriculum. It is a means by which the educator attempts to include a range of different learning strategies around a given topic – all aimed at achieving the same learning outcome – which reflect the different and preferred learning styles of the students in the classroom. Failing to differentiate the curriculum may mean that the learning of students could be hampered.

The curriculum in religious education can also be differentiated so that it reflects the preferred learning styles of students, thereby enabling them to experience success in their learning. There are any number of ways in which this might be achieved. In this chapter we explore three particular learning and teaching strategies which can be employed by religious educators to differentiate the curriculum. These provide a scaffold for the religious educator around which to plan activities that:

- Are challenging and engaging for students
- Address a range of different and preferred learning styles
- Provide opportunities for students to move beyond basic levels of understanding to more complex thinking
- Enable students to use their newly acquired knowledge and skills in new ways
- Use and apply knowledge in new situations
- Provide opportunities for students to practice and master new skills.

The three particular learning and teaching strategies for differentiating the curriculum which will be outlined and explored in some detail in this chapter are: Multiple Intelligences (MI), the Enrichment Activity Model, and Bloom's Taxonomy.

Howard Gardner's Multiple Intelligences (MI)

Howard Gardner is a psychologist who, for a considerable time now, has investigated the concept of intelligence. Traditionally, intelligence has been thought of as consisting of a single entity. Theorists in this area used to speak about a person's IQ, and used an IQ test (originally developed by Binet in 1904) to measure this single facet. The test expressed a person's level of intelligence as a global figure called an Intelligence Quotient (hence, IQ). Gardner's work challenged this notion. He proposed a case for the plurality of the intellect. In other words, Gardner argued that there are many different types of intelligence. Describing intelligence as "an ability to solve problems or fashion products that are of consequence in a particular cultural setting or community" (Gardner, 1993, p. 15), he initially identified seven separate intelligences. Gardner has argued that each of these intelligences has its own set of abilities that can be observed and measured. These intelligences are detailed below.

1. Verbal-Linguistic (Word Intelligence)

This intelligence pertains to a person's ability to use written and spoken language. It involves writing, reading, speaking – using words to express ideas.

2. Logical-Mathematical

This is the intelligence that enables an individual to think logically, to sequence events, to outline consequences, to determine cause and effect.

3. Musical-Rhythmic

The ability to hear and produce sounds is the hallmark of this intelligence.

4. Visual-Spatial

This form of intelligence pertains to the ability to produce mental images, artwork, photography, mapping, etc. It refers to the ability to use symbols, shapes and patterns to express understanding.

5. Interpersonal (People Intelligence)

This intelligence pertains to the way in which a person relates to, interacts, and cooperates with others.

6. Intrapersonal (Self Intelligence)

This intelligence pertains to an individual's ability to reflect and to think, to analyze one's own thought, to be self-aware and mindful.

7. Bodily-Kinaesthetic

It is this intelligence that enables a person to use their body via movement to produce and to create.

More recently, Gardner has proposed the case for an eighth intelligence that he has termed a naturalist intelligence (an ability to perceive things in the natural world) and also for a ninth intelligence that he has termed an existential intelligence. This intelligence pertains to a person's capacity to explore the existential questions of meaning for humankind, such as "Who am I?" "Where do I come from?" "Why do I die?"

The theory of MI provides a useful strategy which may be used to differentiate the curriculum (see for example McGrath & Noble, 1995a, 1995b). The following provides an example of how an educator might use MI in religious education to develop some learning and teaching activities for students in the junior years of secondary school – Junior high school students (between about 12 and 14 years of age) who have been exploring the Parable of the Good Samaritan.

Focus: The Parable of the Good Samaritan (Luke 10:25-37)

Verbal-Linguistic Intelligence

Create a radio/talk show segment or a television interview with the characters from this parable.

Logical-Mathematical Intelligence

Place the characters from this parable on the social ladder in the time of Jesus. What are the possible reasons for the actions of the Priest and the Levite? Compare their reactions with that of the Samaritan.

Bodily-Kinaesthetic Intelligence

Create a movement sequence to outline the Parable of the Good Samaritan.

Visual-Spatial Intelligence

In pairs, create a PowerPoint/KidPix slide show of the Parable of the Good Samaritan.

Musical-Rhythmic Intelligence

Compose a rap or song to represent the theme of this parable (i.e., loving one's neighbour).

Interpersonal Intelligence

Take both sides in a debate about the actions of the Priest and the Levite in this parable.

Intrapersonal Intelligence

Describe personal feelings about the incident that occurs in the Parable of the Good Samaritan. What does it mean for me to love my neighbour? Record responses in a personal journal.

Natural Intelligence

Draw/paint/photograph (by, for example, creating the setting in a sand tray) the physical setting of the road between Jerusalem and Jericho.

Some or all of these suggested activities could be placed on separate cards to facilitate individual and/or group work. They might form a number of sessions of rotational activities in which students select from these activities one that will challenge and engage them. Importantly, the above series of activities requires that students will demonstrate their understanding of the Parable of the Good Samaritan by applying the knowledge in new situations.

ACTIVITY 10.2

> Consider a unit of work for 12 and 13 year-old students on "Pentecost". Devise possible activities that could be incorporated for each of the intelligences in the MI theory.

A critique of MI...

There have been questions raised in recent times concerning Gardner's model of multiple intelligences. Some have suggested that the notion of multiple intelligences is really a reframing of *cognitive styles* into areas of intelligence (Elliott, 1998). Such cognitive styles refer to an individual's preferred way of organizing what is seen, learnt or thought about.

Having said this, MI still has much to offer as a means by which to differentiate the curriculum. It serves as one way to ensure that a variety of activities are planned to meet the different needs and preferred learning styles of students. As a framework, MI also provides opportunities for students to undertake activities outside their preferred learning styles, and so come to practice and master new skills. Table 10.1 at the conclusion of this chapter offers possible starting points for devising activities drawing on each intelligence.

The Enrichment Activity Model

The Enrichment Activity Model is a three-stage model that can be drawn upon for designing progressively complex enrichment activities for a unit of work. It has been used successfully by many educators. For example, Ryan (2001) has used this framework in relation to teaching the Bible. The three stages are outlined below:

Type 1 Activities. Activities at this stage are designed to create a general interest and curiosity among students about the topic to be studied. These activities provide opportunities for a general and introductory exploration of the theme of the unit of work.

Type 2 Activities. The design of activities at this stage enables students to develop thinking skills in relation to the concept or focus of the unit of work.

Type 3 Activities. Activities at this stage are designed to engage students in the investigation of real problems in relation to the topic being studied, for which they will devise real solutions.

Consider a unit of work that has as its focus the life of Jesus. At the senior primary/elementary level (students aged around 10 and 11) a religious educator might draw upon this framework to design the following types of activities:

Senior Primary/Elementary

> *Unit of Work: The Life of Jesus*
>
> *Type 1 Activities (General interest/exploration)*
>
> - Create a class display of images of Jesus, fact files devised by students, Gospel stories, etc.
> - Show short extracts from 'biblical movies' depicting a particular event in the life of Jesus, for example, the Baptism of Jesus, or the Cure of the paralytic.
>
> *Type 2 Activities (Developing thinking skills)*
>
> - In pairs, students compare the particular scene from the biblical movie with the actual biblical/Gospel text. Complete a comparison chart indicating similarities, differences.
> - Design an interview to conduct with the film director in relation to the differences between the movie and the biblical text.
> - Make a jigsaw puzzle depicting a particular event from the Gospel stories. Ensure that this reflects accurately the biblical text.
> - Create big books based on the Gospel texts of events from the life of Jesus.
>
> *Type 3 Activities (Investigating real solutions)*
>
> - Write a review for a newspaper or magazine outlining a comparison between a particular scene from a biblical movie and the Gospel text.
> - In groups of three devise a "Critical Mass" segment reviewing the biblical movie in terms of its accuracy with the Gospel text.

ACTIVITY 10.3

Suppose that a senior primary/elementary class (students aged around 10 and 11) is exploring the topic "Our Church Community". Plan possible activities that could be placed under each Type in the Enrichment Activity Model.

Bloom's Taxonomy

Bloom's Taxonomy of educational objectives (Bloom, Madaus, & Hastings, 1981) is another means by which to differentiate the curriculum in RE. This taxonomy outlines six hierarchical levels of thinking. One particularly useful application of Bloom's taxonomy is that it enables teachers to monitor and audit the types of activities that are being planned. This helps to ensure that activities which involve students in higher order and more complex thinking are included in the learning and teaching strategies. Bloom's taxonomy is an effective means of challenging and engaging students in activities that require the application of knowledge and skills in new situations.

The six levels of Bloom's Taxonomy are as follows:

Level 1: Knowledge

At this level students are required to recall the factual information.

Activities might include: telling, listing, describing, relating, locating, writing, finding, naming, stating.

Level 2: Comprehension

At this level students show an understanding of the facts.

Activities might include: explaining, interpreting, outlining, discussing, distinguishing, predicting, restating, translating, comparing, describing.

Level 3: Application

At this level students use some previously learned knowledge, rule or method in a new situation.

Activities might include: solving, showing, using, illustrating, calculating, constructing, completing, examining, classifying.

Level 4: Analysis

At this level students are required to break information into parts to explore understandings and relationships.

Activities might include: analyzing, distinguishing, examining, comparing, contrasting, investigating, categorizing, identifying, explaining, separating, advertising.

Level 5: Synthesis

At this level students are required to put together ideas in a new way to develop a new or unique product.

Activities might include: creating, inventing, composing, predicting, planning, constructing, designing, imagining, improving, proposing, devising, formulating.

Level 6: Evaluation

At this level students are required to judge the value of materials or ideas on the basis of set criteria.

Activities might include: judging, selecting, choosing, deciding, justifying, debating, verifying, arguing, recommending, assessing, discussing, rating, prioritising, determining.

The following example indicates how Bloom's Taxonomy might be used as a framework for learning and teaching in RE in junior primary/elementary classes with students around 5 and 6 years of age.

Junior Primary/Elementary: A unit focusing on the Church

---

1. Knowledge

Students manipulate 3D models of Church furniture – the altar, lectern, Baptismal font, presider's chair, etc. Complete a matching activity for students to name these objects.

2. Comprehension

Select two features/icons in the Church. Write a short description of these and their uses. Provide an appropriate illustration.

3. Application

Construct models from plasticine or clay of Church furniture and features. Label these.

4. Analysis

Compare two features/items of furniture found in the Church with those found at home. In what ways are these uses similar/different?

5. Synthesis

Using 3D materials, construct a diorama to create the setting for Sunday Mass. Include the furniture, icons, etc., that have been explored.

6. Evaluation

Choose one feature/piece of furniture that you have seen in the Church. Recommend one way in which you might improve it.

ACTIVITY 10.4

A junior primary/elementary team is planning a unit of work focusing on "Easter". Use Bloom's Taxonomy to plan possible activities that will:

1. Differentiate the curriculum

2. Engage the learners in higher levels of thinking.

The learning and teaching strategies described in this chapter are by no means an exhaustive means of differentiating the curriculum in religious education. There are other strategies that can be used effectively in the RE classroom (eg, SCAMPER Technique, CoRT Thinking, SWOT Analysis, de Bono's Six Thinking Hats). Those that have been outlined in this chapter are representative of the learning and teaching strategies that teachers have drawn upon in other subject areas as a means by which to differentiate the curriculum. As can be seen from the examples provided, these can also have a particular application to religious education.

Importantly, the strategies presented are a means of engaging and challenging students as well as attempting to reflect a variety of preferred learning style of students. In many instances, they also require students to draw upon the newly acquired knowledge (the content) and to use this, or demonstrate their understanding of this, in new situations.

Bloom, B., Madaus, G. & Hastings, J. (1981). *Evaluation to improve learning.* New York: McGraw-Hill.

Elliott, M. (1998). Multiple intelligences and other delusions: Gifted children in the Catholic religion classroom. *Word in Life 48 (3),* 22-28.

Gardner, H. (1993). *Multiple intelligences: The theory and practice.* New York: Basic Books.

Malone, P. & Ryan, M. (1994). *Sound the trumpet: Planning and teaching in religion in the Catholic primary school.* Australia: Social Science Press.

McGrath, H. & Noble, T. (1993). *Different kids, same classroom: Mixed ability classes really work.* Melbourne: Longman Australia.

McGrath, H., & Noble, T. (1995a). *Seven ways at once, book 1: Classroom strategies based on the seven intelligences.* Melbourne: Longman Australia.

McGrath, H., & Noble, T. (1995b). *Seven ways at once, book 2: Practical units of work based on the seven intelligences.* Melbourne: Longman Australia.

Ryan, M. (2001). Teaching the Bible: A manual of teaching activities, commentary and blackline masters. Australia: Social Science Press.

Table 10.1. Some Starting Points for Using Multiple Intelligences in Religious Education Planning

Verbal – Linguistic	Logical – Mathematical	Bodily – Kinesthetic	Visual
• Read… • Tell/rewrite a story to explain • Write a poem, myth, legend, short play, news item about… • Create a talk show/radio program • Conduct an interview • Devise a crossword puzzle about… • Write a letter to • Create a file of • Create a cloze activity • Listen… • Translate… • Retell… • Debate • Argue • Review • Interview • Narrate • Discuss • List • Explain • Define	• Translate into a math formula • Design and conduct an experiment on… • Use deductive reasoning Describe the patterns • Create statistics about • Make a time-line of • Research • Sequence, order • Predict • Analyze • Categorize • What are possible reasons for… • Devise a logical argument • Infer • Survey • Justify • Draw to scale • Plan • Apply • Test/experiment • Classify • Calculate	• Create a movement sequence to • Make task/puzzle cards • Build/construct • Plan and attend a field trip • Use materials to show • Dramatize • Re-enact • Mime • Dance • Manipulate • Perform • Find • Role-play • Visit • Walk/hike/jump • Knit • crochet • Weave • Collect • Gesture	• Chart, map, cluster or graph • Create a slide show, video or photo album • Create a piece of art that demonstrates • Invent a board/card game • Illustrate/draw • Sketch • Sculpt • Create finger puppets • Construct • Make • Design • Read a map • Photograph • Film • Match • View • Make a diagram

Musical – Rhythmic	Interpersonal	Intrapersonal	Naturalist
- Use musical instrument - Sing a rap or song that explains - Indicate the rhythmic patterns - Explain how the music of a song is similar to - Make an instrument and use it to - Create sound effects - Compose - Rhyme - Chant - Record - Tap/beat - Hum	- Conduct a meeting to address - Participate in a service project - Teach someone about - Practice giving and receiving feedback on - Co-operate - Negotiate - Interview - Communicate - Encourage - Help - Mentor - Mediate - Work together - Take turns - Persuade - Convince - Debate - Interact	- Describe qualities you possess to help you complete - Set out to pursue a goal to - Describe one of your personal values - Write a journal entry - Assess your own work - State and discuss your opinions - Rank, prioritize - Self-analyze - Reflect - Set aims and goals - Imagine - Diary - Discern - Write a letter to yourself	- Create observation notes - Describe changes in the local or global environment - Devise ways of caring for pets, wildlife, gardens, parks - Use binoculars or telescopes - Draw or photograph natural objects - Observe - View - Monitor - Classify - Record - Log - Link, connect - Distinguish

CHAPTER 11

Assessment and Evaluation in Religious Education

> ### Can RE be Assessed?
>
> The annual magazine of a Catholic school contained the following statement in the section on religious education (which appeared toward the end of the publication after the reports on sports, excursions, other subject disciplines and special events).
>
> "RE can't be measured by an exam but by how you live your life"
>
> - Comment on this statement

The movement over some fifty years toward an educational approach to religious education brings with it a number of expectations. Chief amongst these is the idea that RE should be a subject in the curriculum which demands the same rigour as other subjects. The discussion about how best to teach, what content to cover and how to spiral the curriculum so topics are developed over time are just as important in religious education as they are in the other disciplines. Educational theory and discourse can be used in religious education in much the same way that it can in other areas. A critical part of this discourse is about assessment. Just as other subjects see assessment, in broad terms, as an indispensable part of educational planning so in RE assessment is part of providing high quality education.

This is not to say that assessment in RE should be excessive and without a strong educational rationale. What needs to be recognized is that RE has an irreplaceable role to play in the mission of the Catholic school. This mission, however, can never be reduced to measured outcomes as it aims for the total and inner transformation of the person. In this sense it can be said that the mission of the Catholic school cannot be measured by an exam (or other forms of assessment) but by how life is lived.

> "The special character of the Catholic school, the underlying reason for it, the reason why Catholic parents should prefer it, is precisely the quality of the religious instruction integrated into the education of the pupils". *Catechesi Tradendae*
>
> http://www.vatican.va/holy_father/john_paul_ii/apost_exhortations/documents/hf_jp-ii_exh_16101979_catechesi-tradendae_en.html
>
> of Pope John Paul II
>
> - List all the features you can of quality religious instruction

Looking at Evaluation

In discussions about assessment, the vital role of evaluation is often overlooked. To make a simple distinction, evaluation is something the teacher largely does with a view to improving classroom teaching and learning. Whilst most good teachers have a sense of "how that lesson went", evaluation to be most valuable needs to be done in a more systematic way. This is not to devalue the teacher's understanding of her work. Rather it seeks to situate this in a broader framework that can support intuitive insights.

Evaluation should begin with unit development and be built into the design of courses. As the unit is being taught evaluation should accompany it so that feedback about implementation can be gathered. One of the advantages of unit evaluation is that it encourages teachers to expand their teaching domains by trying new things. One of the reasons that many teachers are reluctant to move into new areas is uncertainty about how successful innovation will be. Planned unit evaluation addresses these concerns in a concrete way by providing structured information on how the unit was taught.

Let's Try This!

Imagine that you are planning to use a new teaching and learning strategy in one of your RE classes. How would you go about trying to evaluate it?

Here are some suggestions about sources of information for your evaluation

- teacher reflection
- informal discussion amongst teachers
- analysis of students' work
- comparison with other schools
- feedback from students
- formal evaluation

Unit Evaluation and Curriculum Evaluation

Another benefit of more formalized evaluation procedures is that they can greatly facilitate cooperation between members of the RE faculty. There is a constant danger when working in a school to work as an individual rather than as part of a team. The tendency to become more isolated is understandable given the pressures facing classroom teachers. By working more collaboratively, however, a number of important benefits are generated. It allows for a sharing of resources so that the individual teacher does not have to develop lessons on her own. It also encourages mutual support amongst RE teachers which can help in sharing the challenges, struggles and joys of teaching.

In discussing evaluation in RE a useful distinction can be made between lesson or unit evaluation and curriculum or end of year evaluation. The difference here is one of focus.

Unit evaluation is based on a lesson or series of lesson whereas curriculum evaluation has a broader focus and often looks at a substantial body of curriculum content. In conducting either form of evaluation a good way to proceed is to ask a series of reflective questions.

SOME UNIT EVALUATION QUESTIONS

- Did we achieve our outcomes?
- Are the outcomes clear?
- How did the students respond?
- Do we have a variety of teaching and learning strategies?
- Is there a clear sequence in the unit?
- Are resources clearly signposted and up to date?
- Is assessment varied and appropriate?
- Was the treatment given to various topics even, that is did we spend enough time on…
- Do we need to rewrite or replace the unit?

SOME END OF YEAR EVALUATION QUESTIONS

- How many units were taught?
- Is there a variety of content and activities?
- Is there a sequence in units?
- Are we successfully building on learning at earlier grade levels?
- Are students being prepared for the RE course at the next grade level?
- Can we revise or replace resources?
- Is the curriculum pitched at the right level?
- Are we catering for the needs of all learners?
- Is our course content current?
- How can we make improvements?
- Is it time for a major rewrite of a unit(s)
- How can professional development be used to improve teachers' skills?

Ways of Assessing in Religious Education

There are a number of significant overlaps between assessment in RE and in other subject disciplines. These are especially evident if we follow an educational approach to religious education. If we see RE as a discipline with the same standards and academic rigour of other subjects then it follows that how it is assessed with have many parallels with other subjects.

Who is Involved in Assessment?

Maki (2010) describes the *Bologna Process* as a key instrument in defining institutional culture. In this model all members of the learning community be they administration, faculty or students have a role to play in developing a culture of learning. At the same time is allows for different modes of assessment to match with the particular needs of a learning community

- Could assessment in religious education take different forms in different schools to accommodate particular needs?
- Do students have a role to play in assessment?
- Does using different assessment modes lead to unfairness?

What is Not Assessed in RE

One can make a strong case for assessment in RE and at the same time maintain that there are some areas in RE that should not be assessed. These largely pertain to the affective or spiritual domain. This is not to say that these domains are not important or that they cannot be assessed. Rather it means that assessment should be primarily directed to the cognitive dimensions of the discipline. In the words of the Ontario Catholic elementary curriculum policy, p.37, " we have no right to judge, in a definitive way, another individual's relationship with God- nor is it actually possible – for much of faith resides in the secret silence of the human heart".

Growing Closer to Jesus

Below is an extract from a student's RE report card

"In the work we have done this year Katherine has shown that she grown closer to our Saviour Jesus"

- Comment on this statement?
- What is being assessed here?
- What era do you think this comment was made in?

> *If You Really Want to Do This!*
>
> Affective outcomes can be assessed but usually involve extraordinary means. Imagine that as one of your affective outcomes you had something like, "At the end of this unit students will feel appreciated and comfortable in the class".
>
> - How would you assess this?

Affective outcomes and the faith based focuses of Catholic schools express an irreplaceable aspect of Catholic schools. To assess them, however, using conventional assessment techniques, like having some type of examination, raises complex issues. Often it is sufficient for the skilled teacher to ask themselves whether the outcome has been achieved. So if one of the affective outcomes is, for example, "it is hoped that by the end of the unit students will fill confident and comfortable in giving their opinions in class", perhaps the best way of assessing this is to rely on the global judgement of the skilled classroom teacher.

Diagnostic Assessment

Assessment can be classified into three general areas. The first of these is diagnostic assessment. This is typically used at the start of a unit or a course of study and the goal is often to ascertain how much the students know about a particular topic or where their interests lie.

> *My Students Don't Know Anything! The Value of Some Diagnostic Testing*
>
> RE teachers often comment that the prior knowledge of their students is poor. This thought is crystallized into the comment "My students don't know anything about…" As a result they feel the need to start topics at a rudimentary level or to repeat course content that was covered in previous years. There are a number of difficulties here. In the first instance this sentiment maybe incorrect. Students often have a better understanding of topics then they are given credit for. RE is after all taught at all grade levels in Catholic schools. Always starting at the beginner level leads inevitably to boredom on the parts of students echoed in the student often repeated refrain "Not this again!" What causes misconceptions about student prior knowledge is an inadequate approach to diagnostic testing. To ask a group of students, for example, what do you know about, let's say, sacraments, is almost to invite a response of "nothing" or something similar. Proper diagnostic testing can reveal the actual level of student prior knowledge.
>
> - Think of some diagnostic testing techniques that could indicate student prior knowledge.

> *A Diagnostic Testing Idea: Who Knows What the Sacraments Are?*
>
> *Scenario 1*: Imagine the setting; a teacher is taking a Grade 5 class. She is about to introduce the new topic – Sacraments. She starts with a question, "Who can tell anything about sacraments?" She is met with stony silence. She concludes that students prior knowledge is poor and decides that she needs to revise her course and spend more time on basic ideas and concepts
>
> *Scenario 2:* Same context but this time the teacher divides up the class into small groups and asks them to reenact the celebration of a sacrament. As part of their presentation each group is asked to come up with three questions for the class that test their knowledge of sacraments. The teacher is surprised about how much students know but she picks up one or two areas that are not as well developed. These are more difficult concepts and she resolves to make sure that in her unit these are addressed.
>
> - Why does the second scenario lead to a more accurate assessment of student knowledge?
> - Comment on how the diagnostic testing above leads to different approaches to teaching and learning on the part of the teacher
> - Can you see other uses for role play in assessment?

Diagnostic testing can also be used to explore other dimensions of education. One area that is of interest to RE teachers is what students are looking forward to in the curriculum and, conversely, what areas they do not keenly anticipate. Diagnostic assessment such a student surveys can address these issues.

Formative Assessment

A second type of assessment looks at how assessment can be used to shape future learning and to gauge how well students are faring in the current course. This is known as formative assessment and can be both formal and informal. It is also known as *assessment for learning* because it is used to shape the future learning of the students. Formative assessment is often undervalued but needs to be emphasised because it provides feedback during the unit and can detect problems at an early stage.

> *We are Having a Test Today…NO!!*
>
> Tests, examination and quizzes are very well-known and valid forms of assessment. They can, however, be used to serve different purposes. The end of year examination remains a staple of summative assessment and is especially common at higher secondary and tertiary institutions. Tests can also have a formative function. Here the primary goal is to assist the teacher to monitor student learning and to frame her teaching around how the students are coping with the course. Many teachers use quizzes in a formative way. This is a simple but very solid way of finding out how students are progressing with a view to modifying teaching and learning to suit student needs.
>
> - Imagine you are teaching a RE unit and as students sit down you give them a surprise quiz. This tactic is always assured of getting a response! You explain to students that you will have a close look at this but it will not go on their report card or assessment summary sheet given out after each term. What type of question would you ask?
> - Would the format and type of question asked in a formative quiz be different from an end of term examination?
> - What are some others way teachers can use formative assessment?

There is Nothing New in Formative Assessment or "I'll be checking your books today"

Teachers have always used formative assessment even if they are unaware of the term. Good teachers have an almost natural inclination to find out how their students are progressing. Good teachers "cover" the room. That is, they are not isolated up the front but engage with students and take a special interest in the work they are doing. A very effective informal formative assessment technique is when teachers look over students work in class. This can be done as teachers engage their students in class or at the end of a lesson or the end of the day when students work books are collected. The key to formative assessment is that it must be done at the same time as students are engaged in the task that is being assessed. If, for example, the students are doing a unit on prayer, the formative task is to find out how the students are faring when they are doing the unit so that if changes need to be made they can be done before the unit is over. Periodic checking of students work is an ideal way of doing this.

Summative Assessment

Summative assessment is directed toward the teaching and learning goals of the unit. It specifically addresses the cognitive outcomes of a unit and how these have been addressed. This is often referred to as *assessment of learning*. Assessment of these goals in religious education should have clear similarities with other learning areas. This is an important part of the educative paradigm in RE. In this view RE should have the same cognitive demands placed on it as other subject areas. So when talking about assessment in RE in this sense, the RE qualifier is unnecessary as many of the assessment techniques used in broader educational circles can be used in RE. This allows the RE teacher to engage with the general literature on educational assessment.

> *Some Assessment Ideas in Religious Education*
> - timelines
> - summaries
> - letter writing
> - work diaries
> - structured play
> - dialogues
> - descriptive writing
> - oral presentation
> - quiz
> - constructing tests
> - poster
> - exam
> - workbook
> - problem solving (what if questions)
> - essay
> - profiles

Assessment Idea 1: Work Diaries

One of the most effective summative assessment techniques, which also has strong overlays with formative assessment is the use of a work diary. This is simply a way of ordering the students work. All the tasks they are required to do in the unit, be they in class or at home, are placed in a work diary and the contents of the diary are assessed. In order for the work diary to be a successful assessment tool a number of important considerations need to be taken into account. Firstly, the diary must have a coherent rationale and structure. It should not be just a "catch all" where all work done, things handed out in class or other material is collected. The students should be clear as to what goes in the diary and the criteria that will be used for its assessment. Not all items in the diary will have the same assessment weighting. Some will be graded in different ways. All of these points lead to the next crucial consideration in using work diaries as assessment tools. The diary must be monitored and given proper attention by the teacher. If this is not done then students will not regard the diary as legitimate but rather where their work, "goes to die." By monitoring the work diary the RE teacher is also gaining important formative information, for example, noting that many students are having difficulty completing this particular task or that one student is falling behind.

Assessment idea 2: Timelines

In historical topics a good summative assessment tool is timeline construction. This provides two types of information about student learning. Firstly, hand it encourages students to get a sense of the whole and how one development followed another and so on. For example, if you were looking at the history of the Catholic Church in a particular country a timeline could probe the students understanding of how that history unfolded. Secondly, the timeline can gauge student analysis of information. This can be done by asking additional questions as part of the assessment task. So, for example, in looking at the history of the Church students could be asked to highlight on their timeline the three most important events. As a follow on students could give a short verbal account for why they made these judgements.

Assessment idea 3: Dialogues

A constructed dialogue is a good way of probing understanding of complex ideas which often arise in courses that have a strong cognitive focus. Take a topic such as the Trinity. The Trinity is a very good example of a theme that while difficult is critical to RE for it describes the idea that is at the very heart of all ancient forms of Christianity. Most Christian Churches today accept the teachings of the Council if Nicaea as the bedrock for understanding who Christ is. At the conclusion of a Christological unit students could be asked to construct a dialogue, and to act this out, which illustrates the Catholic position that Jesus was not a creature but "God from God". The dialogue could expand on how these views contrasted with others at the time. So instead of asking for what the Catholic position is, students are encouraged to think about this issue in more depth by situating the Catholic view in a wider context.

Assessment idea 4: You Write the Test

Tests and examinations are well known summative assessment techniques. An interesting variation is to ask students to prepare a test on all the work that they have done in the unit. What is then assessed is the quality of the test. This technique rests on the assumption that students who can identify the important parts of a unit by nominating them as area for examination and then writing a question from this area have demonstrated a good understanding of the unit. Just as a teacher prioritizes certain sections of a unit when constructing a test, students can make similar judgements about what they think is important.

To give summative assessment structure, assessment tasks are often linked with outcomes.

This is not to say that each outcome has an assessment tasks liked to it. If this were the case then too much time would be spent on tasks which overlap with each other. Outcomes, nonetheless, are often a good way to start thinking about how assessment should proceed. Below are some cognitive outcomes all related to an upper primary school unit on the Eucharist:

Linking Assessment with Outcomes

1. List the parts of the Mass

2. Describe how the early Church celebrated the Eucharist

3. Make links between the Eucharist and the Passover

4. Create a montage on the symbols used during the Eucharistic liturgy

5. Read the story of the last Supper in the gospels

6. For each of the outcomes above design an assessment task.

Hyde, B. (2000). What techniques do teachers use to gain insight into the affective behaviour of students in religious education? *Journal of Religious Education,48* (1), 38-44.

Maki, P. (2010). *Assessing for learning*. Sterling, Va: Stylus.

Ontario Catholic elementary curriculum policy document grades 1-8. Toronto: Institute for Catholic Education.

Taylor, C., & Nolan, S. (2005). *Classroom assessment: Supporting teaching and learning in real classrooms.* Upper Saddle River, N.J.: Pearson.

Serban, A., & Friedlander, J. (2004). (Eds). *Developing and implementing assessment of student learning outcomes.* San Francisco: Jossey-Bass.

Walvoord, B., & Anderson, V. (1998). *Effective grading: A tool for learning and assessment.* San Francisco: Jossey Bass.

CHAPTER 12

Godly Play – An Approach to Religious Education

This chapter describes an approach to religious education for young children, known as *Godly Play*. It has its origins in an approach used for Sunday school teaching, and so is catechetical in intent – that is, it aims to nurture faith. It assumes that children have some connection with their parish Church. Therefore, the most appropriate setting for Godly Play is within the parish context. Nonetheless, the Godly Play methodology has much to offer religious education in Catholic classroom settings, with a growing number of dioceses around the world being influenced by this process, and incorporating elements of it within the religious education syllabi, especially for early years programs. This chapter provides a brief overview of the history and process of Godly Play. It also offers a short response to a series of commonly held reservations expressed by some educators and parents in relation to Godly Play.

What is Godly Play?

As a way of religious education for early childhood, Godly Play is play with the language of God and of God's people – Sacred Stories, Parables, Liturgical Action, and Silence (Berryman, 2009). It is an approach deeply rooted in the Montessori Method which engages the whole child – hands, heart, mind, sense and intuition. It carries forward the work of Maria Montessori (1948), who herself was in fact concerned with religious education (a little known, but true fact), E.M. Standing (1965) and Sofia Cavalletti (1983). It is a process that enables children to learn and use the art of the Christian language system as a means by which to find meaning in relation to their own lives. It is an approach to religious education which is today being drawn upon in many parts of the world, including the United States of America, Mexico, Canada, England, Wales, Scotland, Spain, Finland, Germany, Tanzania, Kenya, and Australia. It can also be found in many liturgical traditions, including Episcopalian (Anglican), Roman Catholic, Lutheran, Uniting Church, and Quaker.

As it involves play, it is invitational. Berryman himself says, "I cannot make you play, because play doesn't work that way. An essential quality of play is its freedom, its lack of compulsion. Do you want to play?" (Berryman, 2002, p. 11).

A Brief History

The history of Godly Play dates back to the year 1970. After graduating from the Princeton Seminary, and after having spent some years as a Presbyterian minister trying find a way to teach children about the Christian faith tradition, Jerome Woods Berryman discovered the Montessori Method, and believed the child's intuition about God could be connected with the language of the church by the playful interaction that a Montessori-like setting could provide.

And so in 1971-1972, Jerome, his wife Thea and their two young children moved to Italy for twelve months so that he could study Maria Montessori's educational approach at the Centre for Advanced Montessori Studies in Bergamo. It was there that he first met Sofia Cavalletti, a Hebrew scripture scholar who, with her colleagues, had already developed an approach to religious education grounded in the Montessori Method, known as *The Catechesis of the Good Shepherd*. This approach enabled young children to hear the Gospel through the use of sensorial rich materials. These included two and three dimensional wood-crafted figures that could be physically handled and manipulated. The children were free to work with these materials that represented the essential proclamations of the Christian message. *The Catechesis of the Good Shepherd* thus brought together a unique combination of biblical scholarship and early childhood education based on the Montessori Method. Cavalletti and her colleagues observed that young children possess a special capacity to experience the presence of God who is already present to them in the inner-most depths of their being. They found this to be so, even in instances where the child had no explicit religious upbringing (Cavalletti, 1983).

Upon his return to the United States of America, and having been influenced by Cavalletti's work, Berryman embarked on his own project, carrying forward the work of Cavalletti. Working initially with sick children in hospital settings, as well as with children in parish Sunday school settings, Berryman developed his approach to religious education, which he initially referred to as *Theological Play*. After a number of years of refining the process, Berryman termed it *Godly Play*. Berryman describes Godly Play as his interpretation of Montessori religious education.

The idea of play is central to the process. But it is not play in general. It is play with the language of God and God's people – Sacred Stories, Parables, Liturgical Action, and Silence. He uses Garvey's (1977) five-part description to more fully explain what he understands by play:

1. Play is pleasurable, enjoyable;
2. Play has no extrinsic goals. It is played for itself;
3. Play is spontaneous and voluntary. It is freely chosen by the player;
4. Play involves deep and active engagement on the part of the players;
5. Play has systematic relations to what is not play, such as creativity, problem solving, language learning, and the development of social roles and other cognitive and social phenomena. While play is not these, play assists and helps to nurture the development of these.

In other words, there has to be an *invitation* to play, not a directive based on power. For a person to enter into Godly Play, she or he must find it enjoyable, and want to play it for its own sake. A person must choose to play it because she or he wants to play the game.

The Goals and Objectives of Godly Play

The goal of Godly Play is essentially to teach young children the art of using the language of the Christian tradition as a means by which to encounter God and to find direction for their lives. Berryman (2009) outlines six particular objectives that help to achieve this goal:

1. To model to wonder in religious education, so children can "enter" religious language, rather than merely repeating it or talking about it;

2. To show children how to create meaning with the language of the Christian tradition and how this can involve them in the experience of the Creator;

3. To show children how to choose their work, so they can confront their own existential limits and depth issues rather than work on other kinds of problems dictated by others, including adults;

4. To organise the educational time to follow the pattern of worship that the Christian tradition has found to be the best way to be with God in community;

5. To show children how to work together as a community by supporting and respecting each other and one another's requests;

6. To organise the educational space so that the whole system of Christian language is present in the room, so children can literally walk into that language domain when they enter the room and can begin to make connections among its various parts as they work with the lesson of the day and their responses in art or other lessons.

The Prepared Environment

In taking its influence from the Montessori Method, Godly Play takes place in a carefully prepared environment, generally known as the Godly Play room, or Godly Play classroom. The environment in which children work and play was seen by Montessori as critical in meeting their educational needs. For example, children from the ages of three to six require furnishings appropriate to their physical size. They need to be able to locate and collect materials for themselves from shelving at their own height.

In a Godly Play classroom, the whole environment is infused with the Christian language system in concrete form, comprised of the materials which make up the various story presentations – Sacred Stories, Parables and Liturgical actions. There are different shelves containing these various presentations – a shelf for Parables of the Church, another for Sacred Stories, special shelves for Easter, and a focal shelf containing the Holy Family (Nativity scene) and the Baptism presentation. There are also shelves containing children's work materials – paper, paints, crayons, etc, and a shelf containing children's "work in progress". Within the Godly Play classroom there will be also be spaces set aside for listening, spaces for playing, and spaces for quiet.

It is important to be aware of the prepared environment of the Godly Play classroom, since it is quite different to most classrooms in Catholic schools. This marks one of the most important differences between Godly Play and the *influence* of Godly Play in Catholic schools. Most classrooms in Catholic schools are not, for a number of practical reasons, organised in the same way as the Godly Play classroom. It is important to be aware of this difference.

The Process

There are six essential elements which comprise Godly Play. Each of these is detailed and briefly explored below.

1. Crossing the threshold (entering)

In Berryman's process, the threshold is important. It is the invitation to enter a new space. The Godly Play classroom door acts in this way. It divides the language and action of the everyday world from the language and action of the Christian people, which is clarified and expressed inside the Godly Play classroom.

The significance of thresholds is often marked in church buildings by the front steps, the special carvings above the entrance, and the like. When people enter, they move from the ordinary world into a new space. The doorway marks the place where one begins to "get ready" to enter this new space.

At the doorway to the Godly Play classroom is positioned one of the two adults who are present. This adult has the role of the Doorperson. The key role of the Doorperson is to welcome and greet each child by name as they arrive. With the help of the Doorperson, children prepare for Godly Play by crossing the threshold from the outside world into the carefully prepared environment of the Godly Play classroom. The child her-or-himself decides within limits whether or not she or he is ready to enter.

The greeting, the friendly smile, and even a quick chat with the child and her or his parents establish the Godly Play classroom as a welcoming space, and one that the child wants to enter. If crossing the threshold is not well managed the children may not be ready, and being ready is important for developing one's spirituality.

ACTIVITY 12.1

> In what ways is this first element of the Godly Play process the same, or different from what happens in a Catholic school classroom? How might this element be adapted to the contemporary Catholic school classroom?

2. The circle and presentation

After entering the Godly Play classroom, the children sit in a circle where the Storyteller (the second of the two adults present in the Godly Play classroom) presents the day's lesson. Circles, as Berryman reminds us, are fundamental symbols. Circles never end. The seasons of nature circle around us. The life sequence of many animals – tadpoles/frogs, caterpillars/butterflies, water bugs/dragon flies are depicted as circular, that is, a life cycle.

Just as the indigenous peoples from all cultures sit in circles to remember and to tell stories, in the Sunday school setting, Berryman argues, the Storyteller too sits in a circle with children. The Storyteller invokes the ancient memories of the faith tradition through the stories of the tradition, and so the themes of scripture become present.

The lesson may take the form of a Sacred Story from Scripture (stories that are concerned with the identity of God's people, such as the Creation story), a Parable (stories which Jesus told to challenge a worldview or way of thinking), or a Liturgical Action (an element from the liturgy, such as Baptism, or from the cycle of the liturgical year, such as Advent). The telling of the story is accompanied by the use of two and three dimensional materials, which are manipulated by the Storyteller so as to model for the children how the story is told. The children themselves will have an opportunity to use these materials a little later.

ACTIVITY 12.2

> In what ways is this second element of the Godly Play process the same, or different from what might happen in a Catholic school classroom when Godly Play has influenced the storytelling process? How might this element be adapted to the contemporary Catholic school classroom?

3. Group wondering

Following the presentation the Storyteller guides and supports what is known as group wondering. The Storyteller invites the children to wonder together about the lesson. This is a crucial step in the process, and it can signal the playfulness present in relation to the presentation. There are no predetermined answers to the wondering posed by the Storyteller. It is not a "question and answer" time, but rather an opportunity for the children and the Storyteller to engage playfully with the lesson of the day. Helping children to wonder about the story that has been presented guides them in learning how to use the Christian language system. The children's wondering emerges from their own lives, their relationships to others and to God, and their participation in the lesson. The role of the Storyteller is to support their wondering. There are different types of wondering for the various presentations. For example, if the presentation is a Sacred Story, a key wondering would be "I wonder where you are in this story…". If the presentation is a Parable, a key wondering would be "I wonder where this could really be…". If the presentation is a Liturgical Action, a wondering would be "I wonder how this colour makes you feel…". Berryman (2002) outlines these various wonderings in relation to the different presentations. He also points out that it is essential that the Storyteller also wonders with the children.

Berryman describes the interaction that takes place between the Storyteller and the children in wondering as "seriously playful". It is serious because it guides the children in learning the art of the Christian language system, which they can use to confront, address, and cope with their "existential limits" (we will return to this term in a moment). But it is playful because children learn what attracts and interests them, and helps them grow. The Storyteller's involvement in this wondering is critical:

When the teacher is truly wondering, the children sense wonder in the air. It manifests itself in the playfulness present in the room. Permission and reinforcement are present to encourage it. When the teacher enters religious language with wonder, he or she shows the children by example how to open the creative process.

Berryman (1991, p. 62)

ACTIVITY 12.3

In what ways is this third element of the Godly Play process the same, or different from what might happen in a Catholic school classroom when Godly Play has influenced the storytelling process? How might this element be further adapted to the contemporary Catholic school classroom?

4. Response

When the wondering concludes, the Storyteller helps the children to choose their work. This may be in response to the lesson of the day, *but does not have to be*. This is "deeply playful work" (Berryman, 2002, p. 56) and allows the children to respond to the lesson and to other events in their own loves. The children may choose to respond through art, drawing, painting, or through media such as clay, or using any of the materials available in the room – in the Godly Play classroom *everything* (including the two and three dimensional materials) is for the children's use and is readily available for them. In keeping with Montessorian principles, everything in the room is intentionally set up to provide children with open access to whatever they need in order to express themselves. Children may choose to work with a presentation they have heard previously. Some children will return to the same presentation over and over. The Storyteller allows this to happen, as those children are continuing to unpack the meaning of that presentation for themselves. Lamont (2007) calls this "unfinished business".

The role of the Storyteller here is to help the children choose their own work, but then to leave the children to engage in it independently. The Storyteller does roam the room "monitoring" the children's work – that is something between each child and God. The response time ideally lasts for at least 40 minutes. In Berryman's own classroom, the response time may last considerably longer. This is so that children have a real opportunity to engage with their work, and to derive meaning from it. During this time, the children may of course choose more than one piece of work – or more than one way in which to respond.

ACTIVITY 12.4

Can you identify some challenges in this element of the Godly Play process for teachers in mainstream Catholic schools? Can you suggest ways in which these could be overcome?

5. The feast

In following the pattern of Christian worship, a feast follows the response usually consisting of cordial, fruit, or biscuits. The children are invited to put away their work and to help prepare for the feast. In the Godly Play classroom, the Doorperson, working with a small group of children, prepare the feast, while the others return to the circle. The feast is an important and necessary element of the Godly Play process, as it, together with the other elements of the process, mirrors the pattern of Christian worship (where the congregation gathers, listens to God's Word, responds and shares in the Eucharistic feast). Where possible, it should always be included.

ACTIVITY 12.5

> Can you identify some challenges in this element of the Godly Play process for teachers in mainstream Catholic schools? Can you suggest ways in which these could be overcome?

6. Leaving

At the conclusion of the feast, the children are again assisted by the Doorperson to get ready to leave the Godly Play classroom. Saying goodbye and leaving are important and necessary parts of the Godly Play process, and indeed of Christian worship. This element should not be minimised. The Doorperson personally says "Good bye" by naming each child individually as they once again go through the threshold.

ACTIVITY 12.6

> In what ways is this final element of the Godly Play process the same, or different from what happens in a Catholic school classroom? How might this element be adapted to the contemporary Catholic school classroom?

Religious Language and Existential limits

As can be discerned from the goals of Godly Play earlier in this chapter, a key purpose of Godly Play is for children to learn to master the Christian language system to enable them to address and cope with the existential limits they experience in their lives. What are existential limits? In drawing from the work of psychotherapy, Berryman (1991) says they are the extremes, or limits to a person's life. They are experienced by all people in different ways and at different times, and they mark the boundaries of a human being's existence. They define our existence. The existential limits to which Berryman refers are death, the need for freedom, the need for meaning, and a person's fundamental feeling of aloneness.

These existential limits are just as fundamental to the lives of children as they are to adults. While children may experience and speak of them in ways different to adults, they are nonetheless real for them. Providing opportunities for children to acquire, use and master religious language in order to find meaning and to confront and address these existential limits is then fundamental to the Godly Play process. While the group wondering in particular provides an opportunity for the children and the Storyteller to use such language "playfully", the response time provides opportunities for children to explore *creatively* how they might use the Christian language system to address the existential limits to their lives. Here, the notion of the *creative process* is important.

The Creative Process

The creative process plays a key role in the Godly Play methodology, since it is through this process that children can confront and address the existential limits and concerns in their lives. The creative process has been widely studied, and an in depth exploration of it is not possible here. However, it is pertinent to note that in relation to Godly Play, Berryman identifies five stages in the creative process from the work of Loder (1981). The first consists of a disruption of a person's circle of meaning, wherein an established idea or meaning is broken in some way. This could occur, for example, when a child experiences a critical life event, such as the birth of a sibling, a major disappointment, illness, or the death of a loved one. The second step involves scanning for a new frame of meaning to cope with the disruption, and to restore cohesion. This step could last for hours, days, months, or even years. Children returning to the same story materials again and again, or roaming the room unable to decide on what work to do as a part of their response could be at this second stage of the creative process. The third step involves a new insight. A new and more adequate pattern is formed and becomes the new frame of meaning which helps the child address and cope with the existential limit being faced. The fourth step involves the new insight being articulated, verbalised and evaluated. Closure is the fifth step.

The creative process is the means by which children in the Godly Play classroom, or setting, address the existential limits to their lives. The prepared environment, which contains all the elements of the Christian language system in two and three dimensional form, provides children with the tools to enable them to use this language system creatively. The adults in the setting – the Storyteller and the Doorperson – support the children in their endeavours.

Kairos and Chronos Time

In a Godly Play setting, time is managed so that the children who enter the room enter into *kairos* time – a time which is both orderly and leisurely. No one will rush them. Both the Storyteller and the Doorperson will tell the children that they have all the time they need. *Kairos* time is not concerned with knowing what the actual time is, or how long the wondering or response may take. This is the role of *chronos* time, or chronological, clock time. Rather, the *kairos* time involved in Godly Play allows for both children and the adults in the room (the Doorperson and the Storyteller) time to see God in the centre of daily life and to reflect on what time is for. Berryman (2002) reminds us that this kind of orderly and leisurely time is the gift that the mystics throughout history have given themselves to experience their own playful prayer with God. *Kairos* time is *significant* time.

Some Common Questions and Concerns

Some parents, catechists and teachers have raised various concerns about Godly Play in relation to learning the tenets of the Christian tradition. Largely these emanate from a misunderstanding of the Godly Play process, but it is important to be able to respond knowledgeably should such questions arise. Two of these questions are briefly addressed here:

> **QUESTION**
>
> Play does not have any real structure. It involves "anything goes", so how will children learn about the faith tradition?

All play has rules and structures to guide it. As soon as one begins to play, one inevitably devises some type of structure to guide the play, even if one is playing alone, or with God as in contemplation. In Godly Play, the prepared environment – infused with the materials and presentations of the Christian language system, provides the rules and structures to scaffold children in their mastering and using the art of the Christian language system (Berryman & Hyde, 2010). It is far from "anything goes". The process is highly structured, and involves children in using the materials and the language of the Christian tradition in their play so as to make meaning in their lives.

> **QUESTION**
>
> If Godly Play lets children discover their own meaning, how can we be sure that it doesn't teach "the wrong thing"?

Ultimately, one cannot be sure that it will not teach the wrong thing – any more than one could not be sure that a book or a well-planned lesson doesn't teach the wrong thing by implication or by accident, as well as by intent. Taken to its logical extreme, undue concern about teaching the wrong thing "leads to a preference for the very *least* effective teaching methods, since these offer the least threat of corrupting the young" (Abt, 1970, p. 115, italics in the original). As Berryman and Hyde (2010) argue, it is dangerous, therefore, to dismiss the Godly Play approach solely for fear that it might teach the wrong thing because such a fear will result in teaching poorly or even destructively. Is this really what teachers want for religious education? If children are using the language of the Christian tradition, and are being scaffolded in their play through the carefully prepared environment, then it would be difficult for the meanings that they discover to be incongruent with the Christian tradition.

Conclusion

What has been presented in this chapter is certainly not exhaustive, but provides an introduction to the Godly Play process as one way of religious education for children in early years settings. The references listed at the end of this chapter may provide you with additional insights. As Berryman presents it, the Godly Play process is not entirely suitable for the primary and elementary school classroom. This is because Godly Play was designed for a Sunday school setting which parallels closely the pattern of Christian worship. The Catholic school does not share this aim. However, and given that the religious education process in many curricula documents has been influenced by Godly Play, it is important to go to Berryman's original process in order to discern the key principles and insights which ought to provide a foundation for curricula that have been influenced by Godly Play.

Abt, C.C. (1970). *Serious games*. New York: The Viking Press.

Berryman, J.W. (1991). *Godly play: A way of religious education*. San Francisco: Harper.

Berryman, J.W. (2002). *The complete guide to Godly play. Volumes 1-6*. Denver, CO: Living the Good News.

Berryman, J.W. (2009). *Teaching Godly play: How to mentor the spiritual development of children*. Denver, CO: Morehouse Education Resources.

Berryman, J.W., & Hyde, B. (2010). A game to be played: Play *and* authority in religious education. *Journal of Religious Education, 58* (3), 35-43.

Cavalletti, S. (1983). *The religious potential of the child: The description of an experience with children from ages three to six*. New York: Paulist Press.

Cavalletti, S., Coulter, P., Gobbi, G., & Montanaro, S.Q. (1993). *The good shepherd and the child: A joyful journey*. Oak Park IL: Catechesis of the Good Shepherd Publications.

Garvey, C. (1977). *Play*. Cambridge, MA: Harvard University Press.

Hyde, B. (Ed.). (2013). *The Search for a Theology of Childhood: Essays by Jerome W. Berryman from 1978-2009*. Ballan, VIC: Connor Court Publishing.

Lamont, R. (2007). *Understanding children understanding God*. London: SPCK.

Loder, J.E. (1981). *The transforming moment: Understanding convictional experience*. San Francisco, CA: Harper and Row.

Montessori, M. (1948). *To educate the human potential*. Madras, India: Kalakshetra Publications.

Standing, E.M. (1965). *The child in the church*. (Original work published 1929). St. Paul, MN: Catechetical Guild.

CHAPTER 13

Teaching Scripture in the Religious Education Classroom

In recent years, there have been several developments in relation to the way in which the use of Scripture is incorporated in religious education. The need for a systematic approach which teaches students the skills of engaging with and critically analysing Scripture texts has been emphasized.

In the previous chapter, we explored a process for Scripture storytelling with young children known as *Godly Play* (Berryman, 2009). In this chapter we explore two further approaches for teaching Scripture in religious education which can be used with older primary/elementary students, as well as with junior high and high school students. The first is an approach based on the work of Australian scholar Barbara Stead (1994), and has come to be known as the KITE model. The second approach was developed by another Australian scholar, Margaret Carswell (2002) and is known as the Composite Model.

Teaching Scripture in the RE program

There has been a significant increase in knowledge, understanding and use of the Scriptures during the last 120 years. For Catholic educators, this has been especially so since the Second Vatican Council (1962-1965). One of the Constitutional documents which resulted from this event was titled the *Dogmatic Constitution on Divine Revelation: Dei Verbum*. It was released on 18 November, 1965. The popular title *Dei Verbum*, by which this document is commonly known, is derived from the dominant Latin phrase in the first sentence of the document. *Dei Verbum* highlights quite clearly the centrality of the Scriptures in Christian life.

SOURCE DOCUMENT 1

Dogmatic Constitution on Divine Revelation: Dei Verbum

> "all the preaching in the Church, as indeed the entire Christian religion, should be nourished and ruled by sacred Scripture…strength for their faith, food for the soul, and a pure and lasting fount of spiritual life…"
>
> # 21

ACTIVITY 13.1

> What do you understand this statement to mean? Discuss your response with a partner.

This document describes the intimate relationship with God that may be experienced through reading the Scriptures. It also emphasizes the importance of having access to Sacred Scripture and its significance for prayer. *Dei Verbum* goes on to state that through

Sacred Scripture, a loving dialogue takes place between God and God's people. It highlights the need for appropriate translations and explanations of Scripture to be made available to assist people to discern the riches of the Sacred Scriptures for their spiritual lives.

The studying of the Scriptures within the religious education program helps students to become familiar with the stories of the faith tradition. However, it must be acknowledged that students in the 21st century were not the intended audience for the Scripture texts. Therefore, in an educational sense, students will need to learn and master critical skills in order to be able to discern the truth behind the stories (Liddy & Welbourne, 1999). In the primary/elementary school, these critical skills are just beginning to develop, and opportunities should be provided for building upon and mastering these skills as students progress through the secondary years of schooling.

In a catechetical sense, learning about and learning from Scripture helps students to encounter God and to reflect on God's action in their lives. Jesus identifies strongly with those who listen to and act upon the Word of God. "My mother and my brothers are those who hear the word of God and put it into practice" (Luke 8:21). Therefore a sound knowledge of the Scriptures is essential to an authentic Christian life.

Liddy and Welbourne (1999) argue that the primary purpose of teaching Scripture in the primary/elementary school context is to develop a knowledge of God's love through the stories and help to build a relationship with God. Within a comprehensive RE program students should be introduced to a wide variety of text types from the Scriptures. This doesn't mean that well-known or well-liked Scripture stories cannot be revisited. Young children enjoy hearing their favourite stories often. But it does suggest that religious educators need to move beyond the familiar stories.

The Scriptures may also have a central role in the prayer experiences of the students. A very important skill to develop in students is the capacity to reflect on their lives in relation to the Gospel. Learning from and meditating on the Scriptures can be a source of affirmation in Christian life and they can also lead to conversion i.e. transforming life to live the way that Jesus taught.

Having then established the necessity of teaching Scripture within the classroom religious education program, we turn our attention to each of the two approaches to be explored within this chapter.

The KITE Method

The first approach to teaching Scripture we will explore was devised during the 1990s by Barbara Stead. It has come to be known as the KITE method. Stead (1994) outlined five principles which she believed were central to the use of Scripture with students in the context of the Catholic school:

1. that students should be introduced to the Bible itself, not to bible stories that are generally so overladen with interpretation and so watered down that it is difficult to recognize the original text;

2. that students' first understanding of the Bible will be literal, and that literal understanding is an essential stage of their faith development, but they should be taught by teachers who have moved beyond literal understanding of the text;

3. that the insecurity experienced by teachers in their use of the Bible with students results from lack of knowledge and understanding of Scripture, not from lack of teaching skill and expertise;

4. that problems experienced in the use of Scripture in the classroom will not be solved by new resources and/or activities, but by teachers who have come to know and love the word of God;

5. that 'how' a passage of Scripture might be used with students can be investigated only after the religious educator has engaged in careful study of the text.

Stead (1994, p. 1)

Stead's (1994) process was designed for use in the religious education classroom with each of the above principles in mind. The method developed takes its name from the acronym of the four processes – KITE:

Know the text	– learn about the text
Inspire the imagination	– imaginative involvement in the text
Translate to life	– making connections between Scripture and life
Express the heart	– prayerful engagement with the text

Know the text

This part of the process aims to give students a sound knowledge of the actual passage of Scripture which is being studied or explored, and the world from which the Scriptures emanated. The first requirement here is for the teacher to have a sound knowledge of the text itself – its setting, the characters, the customs, the speech, the structure and the context. Stead (1994) recommends the use of biblical commentaries to assist the religious educator at this point. For instance, if the passage of Scripture being studied was the Parable of the Good Samaritan (Luke 10:29-37), then students would be engaged in activities aimed at familiarizing them with the *world behind the text* – who were Priests, Levites, and Samaritans? What was their social standing? Where was the town of Jericho in relation to Jerusalem? Why was the journey dangerous? What were the Temple rules and requirements of a Priest that might explain why the Priest did not stop to help the injured man?

Inspire the imagination

In this phase the students engage imaginatively in the text of Scripture which is being studied and explored. It provides an opportunity for students to express their thoughts and feelings concerning those involved in the narrative. Stead (1994) maintains that students' imaginations may be nurtured through analytical questions as well as through art, poetry, drama, mime, and so forth. Using again the Parable of the Good Samaritan, students might use drama, mime or a visual art medium to represent the parable *in light of what they have discovered from the first phase, Knowing the Text.*

Translate to Life

The aim here is for students to discover Scripture as their story – to explore how it might both affirm and challenge their own way of living. For example, if the story of Zacchaeus from Luke's Gospel (Luke 19: 1-10) was the text being studied, then questions relating to the students' own lives could be posed, such as: How might you feel if you had been excluded like Zacchaeus? What would you say to someone who forgave you? Students might respond to these questions through journaling, through art work, or through mime and drama.

Express the Heart

This phase aims to lead students to a prayerful encounter with the Scripture text which is being studied. Knowledge of the Scripture text may lead to opportunities for prayerful reflection and meditation on the text. Centering techniques and guided visualizations may be drawn on in this phase. The appropriate use of silence, mantras and chants may be also be used.

ACTIVITY 13.2

> Using the story Parable of The Lost Sheep (Luke 15: 4-7) devise one activity which might be used for each phase of the KITE method. Plan your activities for students of around 8 and 9 years of age.

The Composite Model

A second approach to the teaching of Scripture was devised by Margaret Carswell and is known as the Composite Model. This is a very useful model and one that can be used effectively with both primary/elementary and junior high/high school students. Carswell's (2001) model is underpinned by four theoretical conceptions drawn from the scholarship of Jerome Berryman, Roger and Gertrude Gobbel, Barbara Stead, and Derek Bastide:

1. That the Scripture text should be first experienced as story, enabling students to think and imagine what they hear;

2. Students must engage directly with the Scripture text. The teacher's role is therefore to deliberately arrange activities so that the Bible can be brought into direct contact with the students;

3. The Scripture text should be actively taught rather than simply used with students. This entails that the teacher must engage in some study of the text prior to their teaching so that their teaching is based on sound scholarship;

4. A thematic approach to biblical teaching is required in which the themes are drawn from the Bible itself. Teachers need to be discerning in their selection of texts to

ensure that those chosen provide a stepping stone in the development of the student's understanding.

Carswell (2001, pp. 8-9)

The model utilizes a sequential three-stage process: Prepare to hear the Word, Hear and encounter the Word, and Respond to the Word.

Prepare to hear the Word

Too often, students are brought into contact with a passage of Scripture on the assumption that they already know where it came from, when it was written, by whom and for what purpose. In this stage, the teacher prepares students to meet the text. Activities which invite the students to "tune in" to the context and nature of the text being explored are an essential element of this stage of the process. Questions around which such activities could be planned include:

- Have we heard other stories by this author? Let's recall them.
- What do we remember about the author? When did the author write? Where and for whom?
- What might we find in a story written by this author?
- Did the author know Jesus personally?
- How did the author come to hear about this story?
- Who were some of the people Jesus mixed with?
- What sort of jobs did they have?
- What are some of the places Jesus visited?
- What can we remember about how Jesus practiced his own religion?
- Why did the author write this book?
- What does the word "gospel" mean?
- What does the time-lag between event and recording suggest?
- Have we heard other accounts of this event written by other authors? Let's recall them.
- In making selections about stories to include what factors might the author have considered?
- The story speaks about a "n" and a "n". What should we remember about these people/this before we hear the story?

Fleming and Carswell (1999)

Hear and Encounter the Word

This is the heart of the process where the students come to know and understand the Scripture text. Where possible, the story is told, preferably with the aid of concrete materials. Students are then provided with opportunities for interacting and engaging with the written text. Guiding questions which might aid this interaction could include:

- Who are the characters? List all the characters – their names and, if stated, their role (include crowds and un-named people).
- What happens? List, in sequence, what takes place. Copy out any spoken words.
- Where does this story take place? If it is stated, write where this event occurs.
- When does this story take place? The text might include the day of the week and/or the time of day when this event occurs. It is also helpful to read the story before and after this account.
- Why might the author have included it? Decide why the author chose to include this text. What does it tell us about Jesus? What does it teach us about God? What does it tell us about how we should live?
- How has the author written the story? Is it a parable? Narrative? Who is the storyteller? Does it challenge or perpetuate any stereotypes?

Fleming and Carswell (1999)

Respond to the Word

This stage provides opportunities for students to express their insights or to respond to the text in some way. Activities which could form part of this stage may include:

- Constructing timelines
- Making scrolls recording the Scripture story
- Collecting newspaper headlines which reflect the theme of the Scripture story
- Researching the Scripture passage using a Scripture commentary
- Constructing models
- Creating soundscapes
- Writing a modern parable
- Re-writing the Scripture story as a screenplay
- Writing a review of the story for a magazine
- Devising dance/movement to retell the story
- Dramatizing the story
- Use computer technology to record the story

Some of the learning and teaching strategies explored in Chapter 10, such as the Multiple Intelligences framework, Bloom's Taxonomy might provide a valuable scaffold around which activities in this third stage could be planned. Others, such as De Bono's Thinking Hats, could also be drawn upon here.

ACTIVITY 13.3

> Using the story of Jesus Curing a Deaf Man (Mark 7:31-37), devise one activity you might include for each stage of The Composite Model. Plan you activities for students of around 10 and 11 years of age.

Conclusion

The models presented in this chapter are by no means exhaustive. However, each suggests a process of exploring and breaking Scripture open with students. None of the models presented assume that the students are already familiar with the text, its origin, the purpose for which it was written, or the audience for who it was written. Importantly also, each of the models require that the teacher will have engaged with the text and will have researched the necessary background to inform her or his own understanding of the text. In the curriculum generally it is expected that, as a part of their accountability and professionalism, teachers will be familiar with the content and processes associated with the particular subject area to be taught. The use of Scripture in religious education is no different. If students are to engage with the texts of Scripture, it is essential that the teacher is familiar with the text and has undertaken some prior preparation. The publications by Stead (1994), Fleming and Carswell (1999) and Carswell (2001) referred to in this chapter are valuable in that they present for teachers the necessary background to enable them to be able to engage with the passages of Scripture and to inform their understanding prior to their exploration of it with students.

Berryman, J.W. (2002). *The complete guide to Godly play. Volumes 1-6*. Denver, Colorado: Living the Good News.

Berryman, J.W. (2009). *Teaching Godly play: How to mentor the spiritual development of children*. Denver, Colorado: Morehouse Education Resources.

Carswell, M. (2001). *Teaching scripture: The gospel of Mark*. Sydney: HarperCollins Religious.

Cavalletti, S., Coulter, P., Gobbi, G., & Montanaro, S.Q. (1993). *The good shepherd and the child: A joyful journey*. Oak Park IL: Catechesis of the Good Shepherd Publications.

Catholic Education Office, Melbourne. (2008). *Coming to know, worship and love: A religious education framework for Catholic schools in the Archdiocese of Melbourne*. Melbourne: Catholic Education Office.

Cavalletti, S. (1983). *The religious potential of the child: The description of an experience with children from ages three to six*. New York: Paulist Press.

Cavalletti, S., Coulter, P., Gobbi, G., & Montanaro, S.Q. (1993). *The good shepherd and the child: A joyful journey*. Oak Park IL: Catechesis of the Good Shepherd Publications.

Dei Verbum – Dogmatic constitution on divine revelation. In A. Flannery (Ed.), *The sixteen documents of Vatican Council II* (1996). Dublin: Dominican Publications.

Elliott, P. (Ed.). *To know, worship and love student text series. Books 1-2*. Melbourne: James Goold House Publications.

Fleming, J., & Carswell, M. (1999). *Sabbath of Sabbaths: God – Father, Son and Spirit*. Sydney: HarperCollins Religious.

Healy, H., Hyde, B., & Rymarz, R. (2004). *Making our way through primary RE: A handbook for religious educators*. Tuggerah, NSW: Social Science Press.

Hyde, B. (2004). Children's spirituality and "The Good Shepherd Experience". *Religious Education, 99* (2), 137-150.

Hyde, B., & Rymarz, R. (2008). *First steps in religious education*. Ballan, VIC: Connor Court Publishing.

Liddy, S., & Welbourne, L. (1999). *Strategies for teaching RE*: Katoomba, NSW: Social Science Press.

Stead, B. (1994). *A time of jubilee: Using Luke's gospel with children*. Thornbury, VIC: Desbooks.

CHAPTER 14

Building a Positive Classroom Culture in Religious Education

"I find teaching RE tough because the kids are hard to control. It's more difficult than other subjects."

"RE teaching to me is great, I really enjoy it and the kids respond so well."

"Teaching RE is different from other subjects; some issues that arise in the religious education are unique."

ACTIVITY 14.1

Discuss the statements above. Which do you agree with? What is the relationship between management of the RE classroom and successful teaching? Are there any special challenges that face a RE teacher when classroom management issues arise? How can these issues be resolved?

There are many factors that make teaching both a challenging task and a skill to be mastered. One of the most important of these, which weighs heavily on the minds of many inexperienced teachers, is managing the classroom environment. The issue of classroom management often has added significance in religious education. Some of the material that is covered has a certain depth and requires teachers to have a clear understanding of what their own position is as well as knowledge of the policy and programs run by the Diocese or other governing body. This can lead to a lack of confidence and ease on the part of the teacher which, in turn, can lead to classroom management issues arising.

ACTIVITY 14.2

Think back to your own school days, or colleagues that you work with today. What qualities do teachers with good control of a class exhibit? How do you think they do it?

Developing a Classroom Culture

One of the most common anxieties of teachers, certainly those who are just starting their careers, is that they will be unable to work with confidence and decisiveness in the classroom. This is expressed in a number of ways, such as concern about how to deal with particular students, uncertainty about how to conduct different types of learning activities, or a general unease about capturing the interest and attention of students. To address issues such as these it is important to stress at the outset that classroom management should not be seen as only a series of short-term strategies. These can be important but many of the things that promote effective teaching and learning can only be established over time and involve establishing a proper and sustainable working environment for the teacher and students. A good way to describe this working environment is to think about it as a classroom culture.

> *Patron of Youth: St Don Bosco (1815-1888)*
>
> Don Bosco was born in the north of Italy and spent most of his adult life ministering, as a priest, to the poor in Turin. He is the founder of the Salesian Order and his views on how best to deal with young people is worth reflecting on, especially for teachers. Don Bosco often remarked on the importance of developing a kindly, watchful presence that was directed to preventing problems before they had a chance to develop into major issues. For him the teacher had to exemplify the virtues of gentleness and patience to be successful and this could be a motto for those working with children in Catholic schools today.
>
> - A saying of Don Bosco was, "gentleness is the favourite virtue of Jesus Christ" – is this possible for busy teachers to practise this virtue?

Establishing Boundaries

One of the hallmarks of a productive classroom environment is a sense of shared expectations amongst students and teacher. Students know the reasonable parameters in which they operate and the teacher does not have continually to reiterate points about what can and cannot be done. One new teacher captured this point well when she commented on a particularly skilled RE teacher she had observed on teaching rounds. *She never seemed to have to tell kids off, they knew what to expect.* In setting boundaries the teacher must have a clear understanding of what he or she considers to be appropriate. This must be a reasonable expectation and in keeping with the general culture of the school. The boundaries must then clearly and frequently be articulated to students who should have a chance to question them. Perhaps most importantly though, once these boundaries have been established, transgressions must be followed up. Students should also have a sense of some rigid, definite boundaries. That is, things that are never acceptable in the class and if such incidents occur they are immediately acted on.

> *Establishing boundaries. Vital Point 1 – follow up*
>
> Consider a simple, yet profound, example such as students continually talking over others when the teacher is trying to explain an activity. This makes good teaching and learning more difficult. The teacher tells the class that this behaviour is not appropriate – *it is important to listen to the instruction, otherwise you will not know what to do.* The first two criteria of establishing boundaries have been met. The teacher now finds herself explaining an important point, *when mixing the paint don't use too much red because it will ruin the poster,* and a number of students are talking.
>
> - What does the teacher do in this case?

In the case described above, the first option is to keep talking but perhaps to do it louder. This, of course, invalidates the boundary that has been established. Alternatively, the teacher may stop and remind students of the class rule – *when I am explaining how to do something everyone should be listening to me and only me!* This strategy will reinforce the boundary that the teacher is trying to establish. Be patient and consistent and eventually the boundaries you wish to establish will become part of the classroom culture.

Establishing boundaries. Vital Point 2 – setting realistic boundaries

Consider again the example of students talking over each other. What if the teacher finds that he or she constantly has to stop the lesson and insist on silence? What may be occurring here is that the expectation placed on students is too demanding. Primary age students find it very difficult to maintain absolute silence and the educational benefit of this is dubious. Why some teachers insist on it is another question but the point here is that an unrealistic boundary can result in on-going and unresolvable issues in classroom management. This can be seen in instances such as when teachers are constantly stopping the class and waiting for silence. Students soon pick up on this *game* and from hidden and distant corners of the room strange and untraceable noises emerge and the teacher is in the unenviable position of trying to defend a boundary that is of little educational value.

Establishing boundaries. Vital Point 3 – review and be flexible

It is important to realise when setting the boundaries in your classroom to be flexible and change when it is required. This is certainly a consideration when teaching across year levels. It is unlikely that the boundaries that are set in prep are all appropriate for senior primary students. Be responsive to students' concerns and demands, especially if they encourage greater student responsibility. For example, the seating arrangements of students can be important to how the class functions. Early in the year the teacher may articulate the view that the seating in the class should reflect the maximum potential for student learning – *I want you to sit here because I think this is a really good place for you to learn and contribute to the class.* This may mean that some students will not be sitting next to their friends. Further into the year when an effective classroom culture has been established some students ask for the seating to be re-arranged. What should the teacher do here? There are a number of options. On the one had this request could be acknowledged but deferred – why change an arrangement that is working well? On the other hand the teacher could trial a new seating plan provided that it does not interfere with the classroom culture. The teacher, in this situation, clearly articulates to the class that the new arrangement is a trial and if it has a negative impact on the quality of the learning environment it will not be persisted with. In a similar vein teachers may insist on a seating plan for one class with a different dynamic from another.

> *Establishing boundaries. Vital Point 4 – be patient and persistent*
>
> Establishing boundaries takes some time to achieve. It is unrealistic to expect students to respond well to boundaries that have just been communicated to them. It may also be more difficult to establish a classroom culture that you feel happy with for one group of students when compared with another group. This is just a reflection of human dynamics.

> *Establishing boundaries. Vital Point 5 – be clear about what behaviour is never acceptable*
>
> Normally the school will have some policy on what constitutes serious breaches of school discipline. In instances where these occur the teacher needs to act swiftly, decisively but not aggressively. For example, students making racist or derogatory comments about other ethnic groups during an RE lesson. It should be a transparent part of the classroom culture that these comments are not acceptable and some mechanism should be in place to deal with students who make such remarks. The specifics of this will depend on the school and how students' behaviour is monitored there.

> *Establishing boundaries. Vital Point 6 – be aware of the situation*
>
> It is also important to be mindful of the circumstances of the school when judging how well boundaries are being observed. For example, the last day of term, in most schools, has a different *feel* to it. What is expected of students on this day can legitimately differ from more typical days. Also when dealing with young students be aware that they may become very tired on occasions and this may come along quickly. In these circumstances be flexible and respond to the changed circumstances.

Recognising What is Valuable

Another aspect of a building up classroom culture is the emerging sense that students and the teacher have of what is considered to be important or valuable within a particular learning environment. This acknowledgment by the teacher and students can be either implicit or explicit. Often what is critical is not what is said to be of importance. More crucial in establishing a productive classroom culture is how the conduct of the lesson gives expression to what is valued.

To give a simple example of this, one of the most revealing indicators of classroom culture is how the teacher begins the lesson. In some schools, and certainly in the past, RE classes have begun with a prayer. This may be in response to the importance that is given to prayer in school documentation. Starting a lesson with a prayer is a perfectly acceptable strategy, but some teachers may find this practice uninformed and unreflective as if the students were performing this ritual in *remote control*. If this is occurring it may be that, despite the school rhetoric, prayer is not actually given a high value in the way in which it is handled within the classroom.

If the teacher decides to begin each class with a prayer he or she is making a statement about the type of classroom culture they wish to cultivate. Consider two types of introductory prayer. The first is done, after some preliminary planning, in a rote fashion. A class prayer list is constructed, students may be given some type of prayer book and the teacher's main function is to make sure the prayer schedule is followed. This type of activity speaks volumes about how the teacher understands prayer and its relationship both to teaching and to the lives of children. What is being expressed here, amongst other things, is that prayer is not really all that important. It is a perfunctory type of activity and one that can be done without too much reflection. There is a strong likelihood that there may be classroom management issues, such as students not paying attention or talking during the prayer, arising out of this type of activity.

Another approach to prayer which speaks to a different understanding of classroom culture would involve a far higher degree of planning and preparation on the part of the teacher and students. This may involve a dedicated teaching block to exploring the topic of prayer in a manner that is appropriate to the age and interest of the students. Students are then invited to take part in developing a prayer roster. The teacher is involved in helping students prepare their prayers and provides suggestions and feedback and helps to provide resources. The dynamic that is created here demands more of the teacher and students. But each party is prepared to do this, as they are acknowledging that prayer is an important activity and to do it properly requires some planning and effort. Put simply, in this scenario, prayer is valued and as a result issues concerning classroom management are less likely to arise in this instance.

> *PLEASE READ THIS*
>
> If there is one way of almost ensuring that classroom management issues will arise peculiarly in religious education it is to use the RE time for a variety of non-specific tasks. Primary teachers teach a range of subjects and are usually homeroom teachers as well. There can be an enormous temptation for the teacher to do other work in RE time. This may include tasks such as finishing off the video from the last class, preparing for the important numeracy exam, or, perhaps most toxic of all, administrative tasks such as filling in the competition rosters for the school swimming sports next week. If this type of activity occurs, then the message that this gives to students is that RE is not really important, and if something else comes up that requires immediate attention then *we may as well do it in religious education*. Whatever the rhetoric of the school, if RE class time is frequently used for other tasks then what is really being communicated to students is that RE is not considered to be valuable. The discipline then is devalued and establishing respect for it is difficult. Myriad discipline issues arise when students understand implicitly that what they are doing is, in the final analysis, pushed aside if something *really important* comes up.

Can the Students Do This?

Many difficulties that arise in classroom management occur when there is a mismatch between what the teacher considers to be important and the way this conviction is acted upon. For example, one issue that often arises in classroom management is the difficulty in conducting group work or class discussions (similar points could be made about role-plays, research based learning, or use of multi-media). Many teachers show an interest in discussion type activities in religious education and rate them highly as pedagogical techniques. Despite this, when these activities are attempted in the classroom the results can be less than satisfactory. One reason for this is that not enough effort is made to translate conviction into a teaching reality. If teachers would like to make use of discussion type activities, for example, have they considered questions such as:

- Are students familiar with the process and comfortable with classroom discussion and debate?
- Are they familiar with using a discussion mat or some other prompt?
- Has thought been given to what topics are most likely to lead to fruitful discussion?
- How committed is the teacher to developing his or her skills in promoting discussion or collaborative learning?

If teachers are considering these types of questions then they are expressing a commitment that transcends the rhetorical and their teaching has a far higher likelihood of not being disrupted by poor management of the learning environment.

ACTIVITY 14.3

What do you value?

Often teachers are not fully cognisant of what they consider to be valuable or important in the classroom culture that they are working in.

- What do you consider to be valuable parts of the classroom culture that you wish to establish?

ACTIVITY 14.4

List some of the other factors that you think influence the culture of the classroom.

- Which are the most important?

"Being a teacher is all about communication!"

- How would you respond to this statement?
- What factors facilitate communication?

Interaction with Students

An aspect of classroom culture that is often overlooked because of its ubiquity in teaching practice is the interaction between teachers and students. For many teachers classroom management is often seen as being encompassed almost entirely by the way they communicate with students. There can be much friction in this area as articulated by expressions such as, *the students never listen to me*, they *are always answering back* and *I get no response from my students*. These types of comments reflect a negative interaction between students and teachers. How can this be improved? Again the importance of developing a consistent pattern of behaviour on the part of the teacher needs to be stressed. Below are some key points about how effective RE teachers communicate with students.

- They speak in a respectful, friendly but businesslike way
- Their tone is reflective of someone who expects to listened to
- They know their audience and speak to students as individuals

These verbal skills are difficult to acquire and somewhat hard to describe, especially the sense of expecting to be listened to. They should not be mistaken with an aggressive or overbearing tone, which are often indicative of persons who are unsure of how they will be received and are, in a sense, already compensating for a perceived negative reaction. A business-like manner is indicative of communication that is clear and concise and which does contain some redundancy. Whilst it is a mistake to think that students are *hanging on your every word* teachers should be wary of long and drawn out expositions. It is also important that students have a sense that the teacher is relating to them as individuals. One small indicator of this is speaking to the student by name: *Daniel, could you please pick up your pencils* is much likelier to get a favourable response when compared with not using the student's name. In the latter case the student can, quite rightly, act as if he didn't realize that you were talking to him.

ACTIVITY 14.5

"I disagree with this. I think that you should talk to students as fellow adults."

- Comment on this statement. What are some of the implications of this statement for communication between students and teachers?

They use language that is affirming and positive

The language a teacher uses is critical in establishing a vibrant classroom culture. Unhelpful criticism, sarcasm and cynical comments are both unprofessional and counter-productive. Student learning is enhanced by feedback that is positive, constructive and informative. A useful point to remember is that a teacher is rarely in a position to make *one off* comments. Primary teachers cannot, usually, walk away from the class when the bell rings. They will see students all day, and the next day, and the next day. What may have been said in a moment of frustration or carelessness may have repercussions later. The relationship between teacher and students is a complex one but it is certainly different from that between teacher and peers. Therefore, comments that may be appropriate to other adults can be harmful to the goal of establishing a productive classroom culture.

They are aware of the importance of non-verbal communication

There has been great emphasis on the importance of non-verbal communication in recent years. This plays a role in establishing good communications between students and teacher. Just as the language a teacher uses should be positive, non-verbal cues should also be affirming. Sitting behind a desk to address students, for example, is a very ineffective way to communicate and does not engender feelings of openness and responsiveness. Behaviours that are associated with anger and frustration, such as pointing or waving a finger, are also not helpful in the long term. Another important aspect of non-verbal communication is the posture the teacher adopts during a lesson. A teacher pacing around the front of a room, is not in a good position to interact with students. If students are involved in an activity that requires movement and interaction the teacher should be amongst them. If a teacher is prepared to move around the class freely and easily this gives a strong impression that he or she is, at the very least, interested in the students and what they are doing.

They welcome and respond well to questions

A key element in establishing good communications is the way a teacher responds to questions. The teacher should display excellent questioning skills. These include abilities such as making sure that students are able to answer most questions that are asked, targeting certain questions to certain students with an understanding of the capabilities of the class and encouraging all students to participate.

Interaction Between Students

An important aspect of classroom culture is the way students interact with each other. Just as the teacher strives to speak in an affirming way, students should be encouraged to communicate with each other in a similar manner. Establishing suitable boundaries largely does this. For example, it should be very clear to students that *putting down* or criticising another student is not part of the way the class operates. If students have a strong role-model here in how the teacher communicates, and a clear instruction about the inappropriateness of some comments, they are far more likely to avoid derogatory remarks.

Teaching Well

> "The students never seem interested in what I say, but if the truth be told I don't actually have much to say."

When conducting an in-service on teaching religious education at a school one teacher approached one of her colleagues and commented that she had just had the worst lesson of their career. The teacher had had an extra, filling in for another colleague who was absent. She was taking an Italian class and although some notes were provided she felt very uncomfortable with the material and was unable to explain the content well to students, answer questions or respond confidently to other issues that arose in the class – which she described as a riot!

- What went wrong here?

A superficial reading of this scenario would focus on the lack of control the teacher had in that class. A better analysis would see the difficulties in classroom management as arising out of the quality of the teaching that was being offered. The connection here is explicit but should not be overlooked.

Teaching well – Case Study One. Why am I having trouble controlling this class?

Some time ago one of the authors was asked by a Religious Education Co-ordintor to help a teacher who was having great trouble controlling his RE classes. The teacher had a great reliance on audio-visual materials in his class. In fact, most classes included videos presentations. Often these videos ran over into the following lesson. The fact that students were restless and difficult to motivate flowed directly from the fact that the teaching strategies followed in this class were monotonous in the extreme. Diversity of teaching and learning strategies results in a conducive classroom environment where management issues are less likely to arise.

Many classroom management issues are related to the teaching that is conducted in the class. This is a large area to cover in detail but the point can simply be made that the quality of teaching can be clearly related to difficulties in managing the teaching environment.

To select one example, consider what is likely to happen if the content level of the lesson is inappropriate, be it too difficult or not stimulating enough. If a sizeable number of students are bored or bewildered, classroom management becomes highly problematic. The way to address this is to rethink the content level of the course being offered. A good many other examples could also be given that make the point that good teaching is a very successful antidote to many classroom management issues that can arise in religious education. Difficulties in this area can become acute if the teacher lacks proper training or background in the discipline. The only long term sustainable solution to this is for teachers, with appropriate support from the school and other educational authorities, to improve their skills in this area. The situation of the RE teacher with unsatisfactory content knowledge is more serious and on-going than the teacher mentioned earlier who is filling in for a lesson in a subject discipline with which she was unfamiliar. The RE teacher with inadequate background could face these scenarios much more often as he sees his class every day.

> *Teaching well – Case Study Two. Why am I having trouble controlling this class?*
>
> A teacher was committed to teaching social justice in a collaborative way. Each session was focussed on engaging the students' own experiences on a range of complex issues – *how many of you have experienced feeling rejected like a refugee?* Initially this went well but eventually the quality of discussion diminished dramatically and students became bored and easily distracted. What was occurring was that the students had effectively exhausted their collective pool of wisdom. They had little more to say. What was needed was some directed input from the teacher on the questions at hand, not more discussion from the students.

Some Difficult Scenarios

After having read this chapter how would you deal with the following scenarios?

1. The intractable student

"I have this one student, Barry, in my class who I battle with all the time. He is rude and abuses both other students and me."

2. Noise, noise, noise

"All the students in my class never stop talking. I can't get them to do anything."

3. Getting too much attention

"Meagan constantly interrupts me and makes trivial and frequent interjections."

4. I keep having to repeat myself!

"I just get tired going over and over things. How many times do you have to tell students where to find the folio paper?"

ACTIVITY 14.6

> Outline a strategy to deal with each of the four cases listed above. Describe your response in terms of developing an appropriate classroom culture.

The intractable student and getting attention

One of the great fears of teachers is how to deal with the genuinely difficult case. The analogy mentioned of a battle used in Case 1 is very apt – and also the nub of the problem. If a relationship with a student becomes a battle then the teacher has already, to continue the analogy, lost it. If one student is occupying too much of the teacher's time and energy then it is unlikely that the teaching and learning environment is a productive one. There are students in schools who have legitimate, serious problems and can be very difficult to manage. These are, however, a very distinct minority. If such a student appears in your class, be assured that this is not just an issue in religious education time. It is a challenge for the whole school community and that is where the matter should be dealt with. The school should have policies in place to deal with such students. It is not the responsibility of the individual teacher to tackle this matter on his or her own. If a student regularly abuses the teacher and other students the school leadership team should take the initiative and provide support for both the student and the other members of the school community. If incidents such as this occur in your class, at the very least make sure that you let the REC know about the student's behaviour.

This type of issue raised in Case 2, is far more typical and needs to be dealt with by the individual teacher. Bear in mind that the general approach to classroom management taken in this chapter has been to stress the creation of a harmonious classroom culture. This is how to counter the type of management issue spelt out in this case. It is important to mention here also the expectation that the teacher brings to the classroom. Often teachers who lack confidence in a discipline can have expectations that are unrealistic and are perhaps born out of anxiety about how the lesson will go before it has even commenced. As a consequence what may be a problem with a few students can soon be described as *all* the students not paying attention *all the time*. To deal with students who are disruptive ask yourself questions such as:

- Is this an on-going problem?
- Is this an issue with all aspects of my teaching or confined to certain areas?
- Do I expect the students to be more attentive than is realistic?
- What do I value in this class and have I started to articulate this to students?
- Have I established proper boundaries that encourage student participation and learning?
- Am I providing a range of teaching and learning activities

Getting too much attention and repeating myself

Be mindful of your language here. The student in Case 3 wants to be involved but is being disruptive by what amounts to attention seeking. Answer questions in a firm but friendly way but also make it clear that there are other students in the class who have a right to your attention. Do not let this student monopolise your time. Make it clear by your communication, both verbal and non-verbal, that your focus is on getting through the important teaching and learning activities that you have put in place. Do not place this student in a more prominent place in the class, or stop the class until he or she is quiet. This merely rewards disruptive behaviour.

As for having to repeat yourself in Case 4, in many cases, this just may be an occupational hazard. Students can get excited and one way of letting the teacher know that they value them and enjoy interacting with them is to ask questions. Also the attention span of primary students can be quite low. Be patient, persistent and realize that eager young students do not always pay close attention.

A Final Word

When classroom management issues arise it is important not to personalise these. Statements such as *I just can't teach,* or *why is it that the other Prep teachers don't have problems,* focus on the individual teacher when this is often not the issue. It is part of teachers' professional life that on occasion they find the classroom environment difficult. This happens to all teachers at some time in their careers. If students are disruptive and unresponsive this is not usually a statement about the work of a particular teacher – chances are that others are having the same problem. Remember to see classroom management issues in perspective. Teachers can be very hard on themselves when what they are dealing with is often part of the tumult of working with children.

Schmack, J., Thompson, M., Torevell, D., & Cole, C. (2010). *Engaging religious education.* Newcastle: Cambridge Scholars Publishing.

Harris, A. (1999). *Teaching and learning in the effective school.* Aldershot: Ashgate.

Joyce, B., Calhoun, E. & Hopkins, D. (1997). *Models of teaching: Tools for learning.* Milton Keynes: Open University Press.

CHAPTER 15

Teaching About the Sacraments

While you will find a brief description of each of the seven Sacraments of the Catholic Church in this chapter, the focus here is also to discuss some of the important considerations in teaching about the Sacraments in the context of the Catholic school. The most appropriate place for the celebration of the Sacraments is the parish community. This is because the parish community is a believing and worshipping community. However, the Catholic school has an important role to play in educating about the Sacraments. In this way the Catholic school works in partnership with its local parish community, and with families, to teach and prepare young people to celebrate the Sacraments.

What is a Sacrament?

In the broadest sense, a Sacrament is a sign of the presence and action of God in the world. Therefore, anything that reminds people of God's presence and the way in which God acts in the world may be thought of as sacramental. Often we speak about these events as being "small s" sacraments. They could include things like a sunrise or sunset, the birth of a baby, dew on the grass, and so forth. These "small s" sacraments are important because they occur in the ordinariness of life, and may, for many people, be direct signs of God's love, presence and action in the world. Many theorists and theologians have written about "small s" sacraments (see, for example, Cooke, 1983; Martos, 1981).

The Catholic Church has, since the Middle Ages, determined and ritualized seven key moments that, in quite particular ways, reveal God's presence and action. The *Catechism of the Catholic Church* (1994) describes these "capital S" Sacraments as signs of grace that have been instituted by Christ and entrusted to the Church. They are a means through which the faithful come to share in God's life and love. They mark the ongoing relationship between God and humankind. People sometimes describe Sacraments in terms of a duty or obligation, but a stronger way of conceptualizing what Sacraments are and what they do is to view them as a gift. They are a gift from God and a call to serve God and others. Celebrating Sacraments is one of the most common and visible expressions of Catholic life. By celebrating Sacraments, Catholics build up this relationship with God. This is most obviously seen in the celebration of the Eucharist, which is the heart of Catholic worship. Some Sacraments are celebrated only once because they have a permanent effect, but the Eucharist can be celebrated daily, so it signifies an ongoing relationship.

The word "sacrament" is derived from the Latin word "sacramentum". This was a term used to describe how Roman soldiers were initiated into their army. From this source, the word Sacrament then came to be used by the early Christians to describe all of the activities in the Church that initiated people into the community of believers.

Because Sacraments can be described as an encounter between God and humankind, it can be said that the ultimate Sacrament is Jesus Christ, since Jesus reveals God most fully.

It can also be said that the Church – the community of believers – is also a Sacrament, since Jesus is experienced in and through the community who gathers to proclaim the Good News, to break the bread, and to commit itself to live as the People of God. By celebrating the Sacraments, the community of believers comes closer to Christ, who is present in each of the Sacraments.

The Catholic Church celebrates seven Sacraments. These Sacraments can be grouped into three categories: the Sacraments of Christian Initiation, the Sacraments of Healing, and the Sacraments at the Service of Communion.

The Sacraments of Christian Initiation

SOURCE DOCUMENT 1

Catechism of the Catholic Church

> The Eucharist is "the source and summit of the Christian life." The other Sacraments, and indeed all ecclesiastical ministries and works of the apostolate, are bound up with the Eucharist and are oriented towards it…It is the culmination of both God's action sanctifying the world in Christ and of the worship men [sic] offer to Christ and through him to the Father in the Holy Spirit.
>
> CCC 1324-1325

ACTIVITY 15.1

> With a partner, discuss and record the ways the Eucharist is described in the above extract. Why is the Eucharist called the source and summit of Christian life?

Baptism, Confirmation and the Eucharist are the Sacraments of Christian Initiation. Baptism and Confirmation lay the foundation of Christian life. Both of these Sacraments have permanent effects and cannot be repeated. In these Sacraments God is present at the beginning of Christian life. The central Sacrament, and the one to which all of the Sacraments lead, is the Eucharist. The Eucharist is at the heart of Catholic life. It recalls and celebrates the death and resurrection of Jesus Christ and the new covenant between God and humankind.

In the Early Church, Baptism, Confirmation and the Eucharist were celebrated together at the Easter Vigil. Those who were to be initiated into the community of believers were Baptised with water (usually by being fully immersed in a pool of water), and then anointed (sealed with the Spirit – Confirmation) and then led to the table of the Eucharist, where they shared in the breaking of the bread as newly initiated Christians. Over the course of history, these three Sacraments were separated for various reasons. However in contemporary times, many dioceses are trying to restore the original order of the celebration of these Sacraments of Initiation – Baptism, Confirmation, and Eucharist.

The Sacraments of Healing

SOURCE DOCUMENT 2

The Gospel of Mark

> Some people came bringing a paralytic carried by four men, but as the crowd made it impossible to get the man to him, they stripped the roof over the place where Jesus was; and when they had made an opening, they lowered the stretcher on which the paralytic lay. Seeing their faith, Jesus said to the paralytic, "My child, your sins are forgiven." Now some scribes were sitting there, and they thought to themselves, "How can this man talk like that? He is blaspheming. Who can forgive sins but God?" Jesus, inwardly aware that this was what they were thinking, said to them, "Why do you have these thoughts in your hearts? Which of these is easier: to say to the paralytic 'Your sins are forgiven' or to say 'Get up, pick up your stretcher and walk'? But to prove to you that the Son of Man has authority on earth to forgive sins," – he said to the paralytic – "I order you: get up, pick up your stretcher, and go off home." And the man got up, picked up his stretcher at once and walked out in front of everyone."
>
> **Mark 2: 3-12**

ACTIVITY 15.2

> What do you think is the main point of this story? What does it tell you about Jesus and his attitude to forgiveness?

Penance (the Rite of Reconciliation) and Anointing of the Sick are the Sacraments of Healing. A person can celebrate both these Sacraments more than once. These Sacraments are signs that God is present and active in the difficult times of life, such as when people experience hurt and need to be forgiven, or when people are challenged by illness. Through these Sacraments Jesus continues to forgive and heal people.

The Sacraments at the Service of Communion

SOURCE DOCUMENT 3

Gaudium et Spes

> For, God himself is the author of matrimony, endowed as it is with various benefits and purposes. All of these have a very decisive bearing on the continuation of the human race, and on the personal development and eternal destiny of the individual members of a family, and on the dignity, stability, peace and prosperity of the family itself and of human society as a whole. By their very nature, the institution of matrimony itself and conjugal love are ordained for the procreation and education of children, and find in them their ultimate crown. Thus a man and a woman, who by their compact of conjugal love 'are no longer two, but one flesh' (Matt. 19ff), render mutual help and service to each other through an intimate union of their persons and actions.
>
> **GS 48**

ACTIVITY 15.3

> What do you understand the above excerpt to mean? What are some of the benefits of marriage for society in general?

Marriage and Holy Orders are the Sacraments at the Service of Communion. In these Sacraments, God is present and active when couples devote themselves to serve each other in married life, and when men respond to the call to serve the People of God as bishops, priests and deacons. Holy Orders has a permanent effect and can never be repeated.

Past and Present Understandings of Sacraments

Throughout Christian history the Church's understanding of the Sacraments has developed. Whereas once the Sacraments were understood to be **things** that were **received** by the faithful to get **grace**, the Sacraments today are perceived as **actions** of God's saving love that are **celebrated** by the Christian **community**. The following table summarizes some of the key developments in the Church's understanding of the Sacraments.

Past Understanding of the Sacraments	Present Understanding of the Sacraments
Sacraments were "things".	Sacraments are actions of God's saving love.
Individuals went to them to receive grace.	Sacraments are connected to life. They come from life, and add to it.
Concentration was on the form of the Sacrament and the necessary conditions under which they could be received.	The Christian community celebrates the Sacraments, rather than individuals receive them.

ACTIVITY 15.4

> Describe a Sacramental celebration that you have observed or in which you participated. What understanding about the Sacrament was underlying this celebration?

The development of the Church's understanding of the Sacraments is important, and classroom learning and teaching about the Sacraments should reflect the contemporary understanding as indicated in the right hand column of the above table.

Parish Based Approaches to Celebrating Sacraments

The most appropriate place for the celebration of the Sacraments is within the local Parish community. This is because the parish community is a believing and worshipping community. In the parish community, people gather freely and willingly to pray, worship, celebrate Mass, reach out to others, and through these activities, nurture the faith of one another. The same cannot be said of the classroom in a Catholic school. While such classrooms are certainly learning communities, students have not come freely and willingly. Although most students enjoy coming to school and eagerly engage with the planned learning and teaching activities, the compulsory schooling laws and legislations in most western countries effectively means that students between roughly the ages of five and fifteen are required to be at school – irrespective of whether they actually enjoy it or otherwise. This means that the classroom cannot be characterized as a faith community. Even though many of the students may have faith, it cannot be presumed that they have come willingly to share faith. Therefore, the school is not the appropriate place for the celebration of the Sacraments.

Many Catholic school and parish communities are today attempting to reflect this understanding by adopting what is known as a parish based approach to the celebration of the Sacraments. The school still has an active and important role to play in parish based approaches to celebrating the Sacraments, but its focus will be educational, and will involve teaching about the Sacraments, while the parish will provide opportunities for the faith formation and preparation for the celebration of the Sacraments. So, what might this actually look like? Consider the following two scenarios from Our Lady's Catholic parish and school.

Scenario 1: Preparing for the celebration of First Eucharist at Our Lady's parish

The celebration of First Eucharist in Our Lady's parish takes places each year during the Liturgical Season of Easter, usually over four Sundays at each of the parish Masses. This year, 46 children – in consultation and discernment with their families and the parish Sacramental team – will celebrate First Eucharist. The ages of the children range from 7 to 12. Together with their families, these children have already attended an "Enrolment Mass" at one of the Sunday Masses earlier in the year in which these children were presented to the parish community. Together with their families, these children have also been attending each of four carefully planned family cluster groups. These consist of a leader from the parish Sacramental team and around five families who have met on four occasions during the evening on Tuesdays to engage in some faith-forming activities focussed on the Eucharist. For example, on one evening, each family was given the opportunity to explore three different Gospel stories in which Jesus shared a meal with others. On another evening, families were involved in composing prayers of intercession which will be incorporated into the child's first Eucharist Mass. A "practice" evening in the Church has also been arranged during which the children and their families will see where they will be sitting, practice receiving the Host, and so forth. The parish musicians who ordinarily play at Sunday Mass will also come to this evening to negotiate the music and songs, most of which will be based on/reflect the Gospel reading for the particular Sunday on which First Eucharist is being celebrated. The children and their families will choose from the four weeks which Sunday and Mass time their celebration will take place.

Scenario 2: Teaching about the Eucharist at Our Lady's School

As the parish celebration of First Eucharist is taking place during the Liturgical Season of Easter, a whole school approach to curriculum planning in religious education has resulted in each Grade/class in the school undertaking a unit of work on the Eucharist. Each unit takes its impetus initially from the local Diocesan religious education syllabus, but has been amended to ensure that a sequential systematic approach across the Grade levels is achieved. For example, the early years' classes are focussing on what it means to belong to a group or community. The middle elementary/primary grades are focusing on meals they share, and how elements of these meals reflect what happens at Sunday Mass. They will also explore how, in the Catholic Tradition, Jesus is present in the gathered assembly, in the Word proclaimed, in the Priest, and most especially in the bread and wine which will become his Body and Blood. The senior elementary/primary grades are focusing on the many Parts of the Mass, and on how Catholics are called to live out the Eucharist. Each of these units of work is planned to have a duration of four weeks, so that it will last for the period in which First Eucharist is being celebrated in the parish. Each unit of work has been differentiated using, in this case, the Multiple Intelligences framework, and assessment tasks have been carefully planned to ensure that classroom teachers can identify, record and gather evidence to indicate what their students have learned in relation to the Eucharist.

ACTIVITY 15.5

> With a partner, use a Venn diagram to compare both of the above scenarios. What do you notice?

In Scenario 1 above, the focus is on *faith formation*. The children and their families gather *outside of school hours*, and with other families whose children are also preparing to celebrate First Eucharist. Family evenings are facilitated by parishioners who belong to the parish Sacramental team. The celebration of First Eucharist will take place during the normal parish Sunday Masses over four weeks during the Easter Season, and children and their families will choose which celebration to attend. Notice that the children celebrating First Eucharist are different ages – they are not from one particular class or grade level. All of this reflects a parish based approach to the celebration of, in this instance, First Eucharist.

In scenario 2 above, the Catholic school has a vital role to play by providing a sequential, rigorous and systematic religious education program *to support what is happening in the parish*. Notice that *all* grade levels are undertaking units of work focussed on the Sacrament of Eucharist. This is because those children who are preparing to celebrate this Sacrament are of different ages and do not come from any one particular class or grade level. *However*, this does not negate *all* students in the school learning *about* the Eucharist, and the material to be covered in these units has been planned to ensure that it builds upon what has been studied in previous grades and is differentiated and assessed appropriately. While the focus of parish preparation is on faith formation, the focus of the school is *educational*. All students can participate and learn about this Sacrament, regardless of whether they are celebrating it or not.

For teachers of religious education, there are two very important principles reflected in both of the above scenarios:

- Sacramental education is "school long".

    The responsibility for teaching about the Sacraments rests with all teachers of religious education, not just those who happen to be working directly with students preparing to celebrate a particular Sacrament. Therefore, the teaching of Sacraments can be considered a "school long" activity that should occur in all grade levels across the school.

- What happens **after** the celebration of a Sacrament is just as important as the preparation that is done beforehand.

Doyle, O'Laughlin and Toms (1994) have noted that while some understanding of the Sacrament to be celebrated is required, the Church has never intended that this understanding needs to be exhaustive. Indeed, it is desirable that those who have celebrated a Sacrament have opportunities to revisit and reflect upon their experience, and to deepen their understanding. This is precisely what might happen in the case of infant Baptism. Those Baptised as babies had no understanding of what was happening at the time. Yet the possibility exists through, for example a carefully planned religious education program, for the individual to deepen her or his understanding of an encounter with God with took place in the earliest moments of life. Therefore, the planning of units of work in subsequent grade levels are important as they enable those who have celebrated a Sacrament the opportunity to reflect back upon their experience and to deepen their understanding in relation to that Sacrament.

The Place and Importance of the Family and Parish Community

All of the Church documents affirm the important role of parents and family in the education in faith of children. For example, *The Religious Dimension of Education in a Catholic School* (RDE) states: "Catholic tradition teaches that God has bestowed on the family its own specific and unique educational mission…The first and primary educators of children are their parents" (# 42, 43). Families educate by being families. While families themselves are not educational institutions, they possess, by virtue of the fact that they are families – the basic communities of the Church – a unique educational mission based on witness and love. Therefore, families ought to play an indispensable part in the more formal institutions that educate children. In other words, "the school should try to involve the family as much as possible in the educational aims of the school – both in helping to plan these goals and in helping to achieve them (RDE, # 43).

In teaching about the Sacraments, then, the classroom program needs to acknowledge and affirm parents and families in what they already do in their primary role as educators in faith. In other words, affirm families as being families. No Catholic school would deny this, yet sometimes the practices of the school tend to emphasise the formal educational process at the expense of the family's experience.

The role of the Catholic school is to support families in their primary role as educators in faith of their children. Some ways in which the school may be able to do this in relation to teaching about the Sacraments – especially if the celebration of Sacraments is not parish based – include:

- Providing opportunities for families to come together to name their experience of God's presence and actions in their lives. The school could work with the parish to, for example, provide family nights (in which all members of the family are invited to attend) both before and after the celebration of a particular Sacrament.

- Ensuring a comprehensive, systematic, and sequential religious education program that provides formal education for students in relation to the Sacraments. This would then compliment the lived experience of families.

- Providing opportunities for parents and families to have some input into the Sacramental program. It is important to ensure that this input is not simply a token gesture, but a real attempt to foster a genuine partnership in faith.

- Avoiding giving families "extra work" to do. Schools sometimes prepare additional materials in relation to the Sacraments to be completed by families at home. This may seem reasonable, but in fact can devalue the nature of families. Families are not educational institutions. They educate by being families. Teaching about the Sacraments in the classroom should complement what is already happening in families, by enabling students to make connections between the content of learning and teaching and their own experiences. Families should not be expected to complete the work of the school in their family time! Families are already busy enough and time is indeed precious!

Consider how what is happening at school might support what is already happening at home and in the parish

This suggests that as educators we need to know both the profile of our students and their families as well as something of the profile of the parish community. This will occur quite naturally if the community has adopted a parish based approach to celebrating the Sacraments. However, if the celebration tends to be school based, the temptation may be to devise the school and classroom program to reflect what educators perceive to be important without consulting families or the parish and asking "How can what we are teaching about the Sacraments support what is already happening at home? In the parish?"

Suppose, for example, the parish community celebrates the Sacrament of Penance in the Second Rite during Lent, or the First Rite each Saturday evening before Mass. Would it not make sense for children celebrating this Sacrament to be included within these parish occasions, rather than planning a separate event at a time that has no connection to the rhythm of parish life?

It is true that in some cases, parents would prefer to leave decisions regarding the content of the religious education or Sacramental program entirely to the school and/or parish community. While it is true that the Catholic school has educational expertise in terms of learning and teaching in religious education, the school community needs to take seriously the Church's call to establish partnerships with parents and families, and therefore a genuine attempt at consultation and indeed negotiation is important. Some parents may welcome the opportunity to become involved at this level of planning.

Conclusion

One of the distinguishing features of Catholic schools is the emphasis on teaching about the Sacraments. The Catholic school has an important role to play in educating about the Sacraments. In this way the Catholic school works in partnership with its local parish community, and with families, to teach and prepare young people to celebrate the Sacraments.

Congregation for Catholic Education. (1988). *The religious dimension of education in a Catholic school: Guidelines for reflection and renewal.* Homebush, NSW: St. Paul's Publications.

Cooke, B. (1983). *Sacraments and sacramentality.* Mystic, CT: Twenty-Third Publications.

Doyle, T., O'Loughlin, F., & Toms. C. (Eds). (1994). *Handing on the tradition – A guide to the catechism of the catholic church.* Melbourne: Catholic Education Office.

Irwin, K.W. (1999). *Responses to 101 questions on the Mass.* New York/Mahwah, J.N: Paulist Press.

John Paul II. (1994). *Catechism of the catholic church.* Homebush, NSW: St. Paul's Publications.

Martos, J. (1981). *Doors to the sacred.* London: SCM Press.

O'Loughlin, F. (2000). *Christ present in the Eucharist.* Strathfield, NSW: St. Pauls's Publications.

Pastoral constitution on the church in the modern world – Gaudium et Spes. (1965). In A. Flannery (Ed.). (1987). *Vatican council II.* Michigan: Eerdmans Publishing Company.

CHAPTER 16

Planning a Eucharistic Liturgy

Some Initial Considerations

Participating in a Eucharistic Liturgy (Mass) is a catechetical activity. It assumes that those who participate are believers who have gathered to share and nurture one another's faith. This is acceptable when a parish community gathers for Sunday Mass. Those who participate do so voluntarily, and have come to share and nurture faith. However, this becomes problematic in the context of the Catholic school when students are required to attend a Eucharistic Liturgy. The compulsory nature of schooling in most western countries means that students' attendance at Catholic schools is not voluntary, and it therefore cannot be assumed that students are either willing, or necessarily able to share and nurture faith. In light of this, some have questioned and called for a re-evaluation of the appropriateness of compulsory celebrations of the Eucharist in Catholic schools (see for example Fallon, 1992; Stower, 1996).

Nonetheless, it is appropriate that Catholic schools afford students the opportunity to become educated in Catholic expressions of Christian faith. It is also appropriate that Catholic schools provide *opportunities* and *invitations* for participation in Eucharistic Liturgies for those students for whom it may be fitting. With this in mind, this chapter explores pertinent elements and considerations in planning Eucharistic Liturgies with and for students in the Catholic school. It begins by exploring the outline of the Mass, followed by a consideration of some key aspects of the *Directory for Masses with Children*. It also introduces some key changes in the revised English translation of the third edition of the Roman Missal and indicates how these affect the *Directory for Masses with children*.

The Eucharistic Liturgy

When planning a Eucharistic Liturgy it is useful to think of the Liturgy as a whole movement with a series of rituals or rites within it. Figure 16.1 shows this flowing movement. There are two high points of the ritual – the Liturgy of the Word and the Liturgy of the Eucharist. In the Gathering Rites, songs and prayers assist the congregation to express unity with Christ and with one another in faith. In the Liturgy of the Word, the congregation listens attentively to the readings from Scripture. In the Liturgy of the Eucharist the congregation gives thanks and praise, and celebrates the memorial of Christ through the holy meal of bread and wine, which become the Body and Blood of Christ. In the Concluding Rites, the People of God are prepared to go out and fulfil their mission in the world. In the middle, the preparation of the gifts is a natural low point which allows people to move their focus from the Table of the Word to the Table of the Eucharist.

Figure 16.1

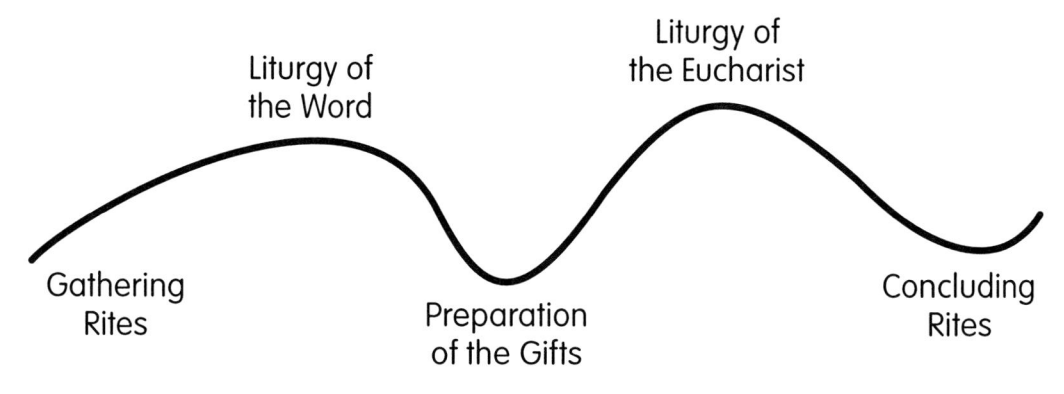

```
                    Liturgy of
   Liturgy of      the Eucharist
   the Word


Gathering                              Concluding
  Rites          Preparation             Rites
                 of the Gifts
```

Healy, Hyde & Rymarz (2004)

Gathering Rites

This part of the liturgy includes:

- the Entrance of the Ministers
- the Sign of the Cross
- the Greeting
- the Introduction
- the Penitential Rite
- the Gloria
- the Opening Prayer

When preparing Eucharistic liturgies for children, the *Directory for Masses with Children* advises that the Opening Prayer is essential; however, other elements in the Gathering Rite can be simplified and varied over a number of different experiences.

The Liturgy of the Word

The Liturgy of the Word is literally a conversation with God. In dialogue the people listen and respond. The congregation listens to the first reading, usually from the First Testament. (Something to note here is that the first reading should always make a connection with, or point to, the Gospel.) The congregation then responds in faith with the Psalm.

After the Psalm, once again the people listen. The second reading is taken from the letters of Paul (or sometimes the letters of James, Peter or John) to the early Christian communities. Sometimes, especially during the Easter season, the second reading comes from Acts of the Apostles. The congregation then responds with the Gospel Acclamation – the Alleluia verse which prepares those who have gathered to listen to the Gospel. The Gospels detail the life and teachings of Jesus on earth. The Homily which follows focuses on the Gospel and the other readings in order to bring out the essential teaching found within them, bringing together faith and life. The Liturgy of the Word concludes with the Prayers of Intercession. Ideally, within the Liturgy of the Word, the Alleluia and the Responsorial Psalm should be sung.

When preparing liturgies with children and young people it is important to take note of their capacity to attend to the Word. It is essential always to focus on the Gospel. It is necessary then only to have one reading; however, it is good practice to frame this Gospel reading before and after with a sung response or Alleluia in order to give it priority. Gospel processions are most appropriate in Masses with children and young people. Non-scriptural readings or paraphrases should never replace the Gospel reading. If necessary, preparation for Mass could include a more student-friendly translation or interpretation of the story.

> **Important note:** When planning a Mass with children and young people, begin by choosing and exploring the Gospel. All other elements will take their impetus and flow from the Gospel.

ACTIVITY 16.1

Look in a Sunday Missal for the short responses before and after the readings in the Liturgy of the Word. What could be some reasons for the differences?

Why do we respond "Praise to you, Lord Jesus Christ" after the Gospel?

Liturgy of the Eucharist

This part of the Mass includes:

- Preparation of the Gifts
- Eucharistic Prayer

Communion Rite:

- Lord's Prayer
- Peace Prayer
- Sign of Peace
- Breaking of Bread
- Invitation to Communion
- Distribution of Communion
- Prayer after Communion

In Masses with children and young people the Preparation of the Gifts can be varied with processions. There are variations of the Eucharistic Prayer available for children, and especially appropriate are those that have musical settings for the responses.

Within the Communion Rite it is important to include at least the Lord's Prayer, Breaking of the Bread, Invitation and Distribution of Communion and a Prayer after Communion. Singing should accompany this Rite.

Concluding Rites

As the Mass concludes, there should be an emphasis on taking the message of the Gospel into the world. This Rite usually includes some concluding comments from the Presider (the Priest), a Blessing and Dismissal. For children and young people, the concluding comments can emphasize the relationship between the Liturgy and life and the blessing can be extended to include responses from the students. Songs at this point should be short.

Eucharistic liturgies are, by their very nature, repetitive. Good liturgy is celebrated in a place that gives it dignity and is conducive to prayer. Liturgy requires repetition so that participants can become familiar with the patterns of the ritual and therefore enter more fully into the prayer. Good Liturgy engages the participants. It is filled with stories and songs, processions and gestures. At its best, Liturgy enables the members of the community to come into union with God and to be changed by this experience. In Liturgy the People of God minister to each other. Liturgy makes present the reality of God through symbol, word and gesture and makes connections between the world in which people live and the Word of God (Healy, Hyde & Rymarz, 2004).

The *Directory for Masses with Children*

Since Eucharistic Liturgy with children should be accessible to them, a document titled the *Directory for Masses with Children* was promulgated in 1973. This is a highly valuable document. Most Catholic schools and parishes have copies of this for use in planning Eucharistic Liturgies. This document is also available online, and can be accessed at http://www.adoremus.org/DMC-73.html .

This document highlights the Church's concern for those who have not been fully initiated and provides guidance to religious educators for the adaptation of the Liturgy to engage children and young people in Liturgy. It acknowledges the need to adapt words and signs to the capacity of children emphasizing that participation of children in the liturgy is a priority. The ideal is not to create a totally different rite but to adapt and make the liturgical elements more appropriate for the young people who gather.

Chapter One emphasizes the strong connection between liturgical and Eucharistic formation and the general education of young people.

> Children should experience and respond to the human values inherent in the Eucharist…community activity, exchange of greetings, capacity to listen and to seek and grant pardon, expression of gratitude, experience of symbolic actions, meal of friendship, festive celebration. (# 9)

ACTIVITY 16.2

Access the Directory for Masses with Children at: http://www.adoremus.org/DMC-73.html

Chapter Two of the Directory deals with Masses with adults in which children also participate. List three ways that a community could encourage active and conscious participation in the liturgy.

Share other ideas you have experienced from parishes you have visited.

ACTIVITY 16.3

Access the Directory for Masses with Children at:

http://www.adoremus.org/DMC-73.html

Chapter Three deals with Masses with children in which only a few adults participate. Identify directions which may promote learning in the different liturgical elements. Discuss with colleagues and list ways as a teacher you might promote learning for liturgy in your classroom program.

> **Important note:** The table at the end of this chapter presents a summary of the adaptations outlined in the *Directory for Masses with Children* which may be drawn upon in planning Eucharistic celebrations with children. The schema was originally compiled by Fr Peter Conroy, a priest of the Archdiocese of Melbourne.

The Revised English Translation of the Third Edition of the Roman Missal

In the last few years the revised English translation of the third edition of the *Roman Missal* has been completed. The Holy See approved the new translation with the required recognitio in March 2010, and it has been promulgated for use and introduced into different countries and diocese since that time. For instance, its use in Australia was promulgated on Pentecost Sunday, 2011. For the most part, the revised translation is not wholly different, although there are one or two notable differences, particularly in relation some of the congregation's responses. For instance, the following table presents two notable examples of the revised translation.

Table 16.1: Some examples of the revised translation

Familiar Translation	Revised Translation
Priest: The Lord be with you Congregation: And also with you	Priest: The Lord be with you Congregation: And with your spirit
Congregation: Holy, Holy, Holy Lord God of power and might	Congregation: Holy, Holy, Holy Lord God of Hosts

With the promulgation of the new text, the first change Catholics hear in the revised translation of the *Order of Mass* is the response to the priest's greeting: "The Lord be with you." The new response: "and with your spirit." The familiar text for the first line of the *Sanctus* is translated as "Holy, holy, holy Lord, God of power and might." The phrase "power and might" is not a literal translation from the Latin, "*Sanctus, sanctus, sanctus Dominus Deus sabaoth.*" "Sabaoth" is a transliteration of the Hebrew *Tz'vaot* meaning "armies or hosts." The revised version now reads "Holy, Holy, Holy Lord God of hosts," which is closer to the rendering of Isaiah 6:3 found in several translation of the Bible.

In addition to the literal translation of the *Sanctus* and *et cum spiritu tuo*, the text "through my fault, through my fault, through my most grievous fault" has been added to the *Confiteor*. There are also word changes in the *Gloria* that are closer to the Latin text and Latin word order (syntax). Also, the translation of the Preface dialogue's *Dignum et justum est* is "It is right and just." Following the institution narrative, the priest now says: "The mystery of faith." The assembly then acclaims one of newly translated acclamations. It should be noted that the familiar "Christ has died, Christ is risen, Christ will come again" (formerly known as Memorial Acclamation A) is no longer one of the approved acclamations. The revised response of the people to the *Ecce Agnus Dei*, "Behold the Lamb of God" is "Lord, I am not worthy that you should enter under my roof, but only say the word and my soul shall be healed." Many other text revisions concern only the prayers (collects) and ritual words recited by the priest.

Directory for Masses with Children and the Revised Roman Missal

In liturgies where the *Directory for Masses with Children* is followed and children are in the majority, a celebrant can still choose from the introductory elements of the Mass and, at times, eliminate the penitential act and/or Gloria all together. In the new *Order of Mass* there are textual changes in Form A and B of the penitential act, including the additions to the *Confiteor* mentioned above. As an introductory element with children, a penitential act would seem appropriate during Lent, the Gloria during the Christmas season and the rite of sprinkling during the Easter season. The priest is also permitted to choose from the *Roman Missal* presidential prayers more suited to children and may even adapt the text of those prayers to the needs of children. Children are encouraged to learn the Nicene Creed, but the Directory allows for the use of the Apostles' Creed when a creed is desired in Masses with children.

The *Eucharistic Prayers for Children* are not a part of the new *Roman Missal*. It remains to be seen if and when they will be revised. Although it is a completely separate liturgical book, the revision of the *Lectionary for Masses with Children* is in the same position as the Eucharistic prayers. In the meantime, both the children's Eucharistic prayers and the children's Lectionary can still be used. Many celebrants are successful in helping children to focus on the Eucharistic prayer by suggesting reasons for giving thanks before beginning the dialogue of the preface.

While the *Directory for Masses with Children* allows for children to sing acclamations with words that differ from the official texts, most choir directors and liturgists who work regularly with children try to use acclamations and Mass settings that are commonly heard in the parish Sunday liturgies.

An excellent resource that can assist those planning Liturgies for children and young people using the *Directory for Masses with Children* and the revised translation of the Roman Missal has been written by liturgist Jack Miffleton, titled *Today's Liturgy with Children*. It can be accessed online at http://www.ocp.org/articles/1227.

Some Other Considerations

In planning Masses with children and young people, there are several other considerations which need to be taken into account. These are listed below:

1. *Children who have not yet celebrated First Eucharist*. If you are planning a Mass in which **most** of the participants will be children who have not yet celebrated their First Eucharist, consider whether it might be more appropriate to plan a *non-Eucharistic celebration* (for an outline of such celebrations, see Hyde & Rymarz, 2008). A Eucharistic celebration with such children effectively means that they cannot participate fully. It is like leading them to the table, and then turning them away hungry.

2. *The environment in which the Eucharistic celebration will take place*. The most appropriate environment is, of course, the parish church. However, in some cases, this may not be practical. For instance, if just one class has been invited to celebrate the Eucharist, and the parish church is not in the school grounds, it may be that an alternative venue needs to be sought. If the venue is not going to be the parish church, then questions such as the following need to be addressed: *Is the chosen environment conducive to prayer? How can an ambiance be created? Will the layout of the space allow room for procession and gesture? Can I subdue the lighting? Is the space comfortable?*

3. *A prayer focus*. It may be appropriate to create a focus point around the theme of the Eucharist which will centre the students. For example, if the theme for the Eucharistic celebration was "discipleship", and the Gospel reading was Jesus calling the first disciples, then it may be appropriate to design a small focus which could consist of fishing net and some sandals.

4. *Music and song.* If music is to be used, what type? If singing is to occur, appropriate hymns should be used which reflect the theme of the Eucharistic Liturgy. Will these be recorded or can the students use instruments or simply their own voices? There is a plethora of excellent children's liturgical music compilations, composed by experienced musicians and liturgists, which are readily accessible and which can be purchased through world-wide distributors. It may also be appropriate to include soft music, or even periods of silence.

5. *Time.* Allow sufficient time for students to enter the experience of the Eucharistic Liturgy. Don't rush things. Do not be afraid of periods of silence to slow the tempo down.

6. *Reading.* If students are to read, they need to be prepared and practiced. Teach students to slow their reading, and allow them enough time prior to the celebration to practice and master this skill.

7. *The Presider (the Priest).* Make sure that you have consulted with the priest who is presiding at the Eucharistic Liturgy **beforehand**. Many priests will want to see and approve a planned outline of the theme for the Mass well in advance of the celebration. Some parish priests are more liberal in what they will allow to occur during a Eucharistic celebration than are others. It is imperative that you consult and, where possible, include the priest in your planning.

> **Important note:** When celebrating Mass in which there are mostly children present, the *Directory for Masses with Children* indicates that during the homily someone other than the priest may speak.

Conclusion

In this chapter we have presented an outline of the elements of a Eucharistic celebration, and we have examined some of the principles of good liturgical preparation guided by the *Directory for Masses with Children*. It also introduced some key changes in the revised English translation of the third edition of the Roman Missal and indicated how these affect the *Directory for Masses with Children*. It must be reiterated that participation in the Eucharist must be invitational, since it is catechetical by its nature. That is, participation in Mass assumes those who make up the congregation have come of their own free will, and are ready, willing and able to share and nurture one another in faith. Having made this point, it is appropriate that Catholic primary schools afford students the opportunity to become educated in Catholic expressions of Christian faith, and that they provide *opportunities* and *invitation* for participation in Eucharist Liturgies for those students for whom it may be fitting.

Attfield, D. (1990). Presenting the Eucharist in a primary school. *British Journal of Religious Education, 12* (3), 167-171.

Canadian Conference of Catholic Bishops. (1996). *Directory for Masses with Children, with Index.* (New Edition). Ottawa: Canadian Conference of Catholic Bishops.

Fallon, M. (1992). Celebrating Eucharist between school and parish. *Liturgy News, 22* (2), 2-5.

Healy, H., Hyde, B., & Rymarz, R. (2004). *Making our way through primary RE: A handbook for religious educators.* Tuggerah, NSW: Social Science Press.

Hyde, B., & Rymarz, R. (2008). *First steps in religious education.* Ballan, VIC: Connor Court Publishing.

Miffleton, J. (2010). *Today's Liturgy with Children.* Accessed online at http://www.ocp.org/articles/1227.

Stower, L. (1996). Celebrating Eucharist in Australian Catholic primary schools: Towards a statement of policy and practice. *Word In Life,* August, 10-15.

Sacred Congregation for Catholic Education. (1997). *General directory for catechesis.* Homebush: St Paul's Publications.

The Holy See. (1994). *Catechism of the Catholic Church.* Homebush: St Paul's Publications.

Preparing the Eucharistic Liturgy for Children

INTRODUCTORY RITES		LITURGY OF THE WORD	
MISSAL	**DMC**	**MISSAL**	**DMC**
Entrance of Minister Sign of Cross Greeting Introduction Penitential Rite Lord Have Mercy Gloria (Sundays) Opening Prayer	At least – Opening prayer and one other element, to be varied over a number of celebrations	1st Reading Psalm Response 2nd Reading Acclamation Gospel Homily Creed (Sundays) Intercessions	At least – Gospel, perhaps framed with a sung response or acclamation Some response (silence) Homily (some person other than priest may speak) During the Liturgy the Scriptures should be read Intercessions

LITURGY OF THE EUCHARIST		CONCLUDING RITES	
MISSAL	**DMC**	**MISSAL**	**DMC**
Preparation of Gifts Eucharistic Prayer Communion Rite Lord's Prayer Peace Prayer Sign of Peace Breaking of Bread Invitation to Communion Distribution Prayer	At least – Preparation of Gifts Eucharistic Prayer (children's) Communion Rite At least – Lord's Prayer Breaking of Bread Invitation to Communion Distribution with procession song Prayer	Concluding comments Blessing Dismissal	Concluding comments relating the Liturgy to life Extended blessing Dismissal

This schema was originally compiled by Fr Peter Conroy, a priest of the Archdiocese of Melbourne. The authors acknowledge this work.

CHAPTER 17

Some Challenges in Teaching Religious Education

QUESTIONS

1. Do you have any general concerns about your teaching career?
2. What, if any, were your experiences of religious education in school?
3. What is your attitude to teaching religious education?

Many new teachers can be anxious about how they will cope in the classroom. Many teachers, especially inexperienced ones, often have an exaggerated fear about the problems that may arise in RE. In a school with a well-thought-out and implemented RE curriculum and where the teachers are well versed in their professional responsibilities the focus of classroom RE tends to be on meeting educational goals. By having this focus, problems that arise can be dealt with within the context of the ethos of Catholic schools. By understanding some of the issues that may arise and how to respond well, the new RE teacher can work with confidence in the classroom and in the wider school. If teachers are prepared to discuss their concerns when they arise with the relevant people in the school, be they the Religious Education Coordinator (REC) or members of the school's leadership team, then difficulties can be minimised.

QUESTIONS

1. In your experience of Catholic schools what are some of the difficulties that arise in RE classes?
2. How would you rank these in terms of seriousness?
3. Which are the most frequent?

Talking Things Over

Casey: *I am really looking forward to teaching, but RE worries me a bit. I'm just not confident; I mean, I don't know anything about it.*

Teagan: *Yeah, me too. I mean, what are sacraments and all the other stuff? What are we supposed to do?*

Casey: *I'm not sure what place we give Church teaching.*

Sam: *What about some of the questions the kids can ask? I just wouldn't know what to say.*

Lucas: *And there are also lifestyle issues; how much of it are you supposed to take personally?*

Sarah: *I've heard that schools check up on you to see how you are living.*

Kate: *Don't get too paranoid. Schools respect your private life as long as you keep it private. What they are interested in is how you teach and interact with students.*

Teagan: *Schools are really learning focused. I'm sure once you get into schools there will be lots of assistance available.*

Casey: *I think you're right. When I was doing my observations the school was great and gave the new teachers terrific support, especially in RE.*

Lucas: *Gee, I don't think so. At the school I was at RE didn't seem to work at all. There was not a lot of quality teaching and learning going on. The RE teaching was just not challenging. I just couldn't figure out what they were doing. Each teacher was doing her own thing and not following any curriculum.*

Marina: *What if you make a mistake and get parents calling in and giving you a hard time?*

Imagine that you are listening to this conversation. Who do you most identify with?

Issue Number 1: Content knowledge and RE – *I just don't know anything about it*

In the dialogue above Casey expressed that her greatest anxiety about teaching RE was a lack of content knowledge. Teagan agreed with her. This is a good example of an issue that troubles many new RE teachers. In recent years classroom RE teaching has placed more emphasis on the educational goals of RE. If you want to help students understand more about the Catholic tradition, or any other for that matter, then you need to have a strong grasp of the content of RE. There is no way of avoiding this. If, for example, you are involved in teaching about a sacramental program, you need to have a good grasp of the theology behind the Eucharist in order to convey this to students.

If the RE teacher wants to teach well within an educational approach they must prepare themselves with background information about the topics they are teaching. This is especially true when teachers take upon themselves the responsibility of speaking for the Tradition. Casey expresses concerns in this area. It is very necessary for RE teachers to understand Church teachings and to be able to explain them. When a teacher, for example, says *the Catholic Church teaches …* he or she is making an objective statement. And these go to the heart of the content domain in religious education in Catholic schools as they set out the framework for Catholic belief and practise. Statements on Church teaching should be encouraged because they give students a firm position on which their own understanding can grow. It is the responsibility, nonetheless, of the RE teacher to be accurate when making objective statements. If unsure about statements on behalf of the Tradition check with other suitably qualified people. Rymarz (2012a) puts this view in the following terms:

> *The official teaching of the Church – or the Church's story – [in Catholic schools] is presented as a normative position and the teacher's task is to present this in an educationally sophisticated way. This does seem to be a consistent position and within the bounds of religious education in a Catholic school. The Catholic Church, along with other major religious faiths, has always claimed for itself the right to define its own beliefs and practices. Students and parents who are part of the community of Catholic schools are entitled to a religious education where the positions of the*

Catholic Church are clearly stated. This does not mean that other views are not put but it does offer the official Church teaching a special place in the curriculum.

Teachers should do their homework thoroughly before approaching a new or unfamiliar topic. They need to approach complex issues with caution. They can get into some difficulty by launching into areas which require careful preparation and background reading. To be prepared does not mean that to teach RE well you need to have a post-graduate qualification in theology, scripture or religious education. This is not to say these would not help, and many teachers take on extra studies to improve their knowledge base. Most senior teachers have such post-graduate qualifications or are in the process of getting them. In many dioceses this is required to take up a leadership position in RE. Classroom teachers, especially early in their career, can gain a good insight into topics by directed reading. Most RE curricula have notes for teachers which distil much of the main points in the area. Be prepared also to speak to the leadership team at the school for what assistance is available at the school level.

Issue Number 2: What would you do if a student asked a hard but legitimate question in the RE class?

You could also put the issue that Sam raises under the heading of content knowledge.

Students can ask some really tough questions. 'Is this wrong?', 'Why does God let this happen?', and 'Did Adam and Eve really exist?' are some examples. If students ask you questions then take this as a compliment. Research shows that students do this when they have some faith in your ability as a teacher and feel comfortable in your presence. It also means that it is likely that you have created a strong learning environment in your classroom. Some of the questions that come up in RE are complex. Do not feel that you have to come up with all the answers to the great questions of life. It is acceptable to take some questions 'on notice' and get back to students. As your confidence grows and your understanding of content areas improves you will find that you can give students credible answers to many questions.

Other questions may arise spontaneously on issues that are topical at the time. These may come up in the electronic media and hence have a very wide circulation. One example of such material is the issue of clerical sexual abuse. How should an inexperienced RE teacher deal with issues like this? If discussion arises in the course of a lesson some further comment is appropriate. Certainly an expression of sorrow and an acknowledgment of the deep hurt that has been caused can be made. Depending on the age of the students some deeper analysis can also be given. There is, however, no easy answer to many current and topical issues. It is unlikely that discussing them at great length will assist in resolution or significant progress. There is also the danger that the purposeful teaching of the RE curriculum will be disrupted if too much attention is given to issues as they arise. The RE teacher should be responsive to student enquiries about issues of the day; however, this should not become the main focus of the RE classroom. It is not advisable to allow the RE classroom to become dominated by discussion of issues that have arisen in the most recent blockbuster movie or segment on current affairs shows. Ideally many of these topics could be discussed within the existing RE curriculum where they can be placed in an appropriate educational context.

Issue Number 3: Help at the school – *I'm sure once you get into schools there will be lots of assistance available.*

In the dialogue above Casey and Lucas have different experiences of the amount of support given to new RE teachers in schools. Fortunately, Casey's experience is the norm. Most schools have a strong commitment to RE and do a good deal to help teachers, especially those who are new to the profession. Most schools have experienced teachers in leadership positions in RE. This person is usually the REC or someone in a similar position. Part of their job is to help RE teachers, and this includes new staff when the need arises. New RE teachers can make situations more difficult for themselves if they do not communicate regularly with the REC. Some issues that arise in the contemporary RE class can be difficult for an inexperienced teacher to deal with alone. These are not problems, however, that occur in isolation, and are dealt with on a school basis. They have been faced before and can be dealt with effectively provided concerned parties are informed about what is going on.

Issue Number 4: Expectations of parents – *What if you make a mistake and get parents calling in and giving you a hard time?*

The basic advice here is to make sure that you are familiar with the school's RE program, and if difficulties arise promptly inform the REC or faculty leader. Difficulties here could include being contacted by a parent directly about something that has occurred in your RE class. A parent, for example, may raise concerns over the sacramental program and suggest that the children are being presented something which is contrary to Catholic teaching. Or another parent may want the school to keep up with the times and teach something which is not in accord with the Catholic tradition. It is important for the new RE teacher to be aware that the religious education program in the school is not something that is fashioned by the school alone. In Catholic schools the RE program is controlled and authorised, ultimately, by the bishop. In the Catholic tradition it is the bishop, not the teacher or the parent, who is the final authority on whether something conforms to Catholic teaching or not. Teachers working in Catholic schools can be confident that what is in the school's religious education curriculum conforms to Catholic teaching because it has been approved by the bishop through official educational agencies which work under his mandate. Because of this parents cannot ask the school to present material in religious education that is not in accord with what the Church teaches.

Bear in mind that if parents express an interest in what goes on in the RE class this is a positive thing. If misunderstandings occur they can usually be corrected with better communication. Parents with obvious interest in the religious education of their child should be encouraged and welcomed. Consulting with the parent usually results in a satisfactory outcome.

Issue Number 5: Professional responsibilities and the private lives of RE teachers – lifestyle issues, how much of it are you supposed to take personally?

Lucas has raised the issue of the relationship between the professional and personal lives of RE teachers. What are the boundaries of the personal lives of RE teachers? This question is not restricted to RE, but affects all teachers who work in Catholic schools.

QUESTIONS

1. What do you see as the boundaries around the personal life of the teacher?
2. What are some of the issues that are brought up by this case?

SOURCE DOCUMENT 1

Lay Catholics in Schools: Witnesses to Faith

> The teacher under discussion here is not simply a professional person who systematically transmits a body of knowledge in the context of a school; 'teacher' is to be understood as 'educator' – one who helps to form human persons. The task of a teacher goes well beyond transmission of knowledge, although that is not excluded. Therefore, if adequate professional preparation is required in order to transmit knowledge, then adequate professional preparation is even more necessary in order to fulfill the role of a genuine teacher. It is an indispensable human formation, and without it, it would be foolish to undertake any educational work.
>
> One specific characteristic of the educational profession assumes its most profound significance in the Catholic educator: the communication of truth. For the Catholic educator, whatever is true is a participation in Him who is the Truth; the communication of truth, therefore, as a professional activity, is thus fundamentally transformed into a unique participation in the prophetic mission of Christ, carried on through one's teaching.
>
> LCS: WF 16

QUESTIONS

1. What implications does this extract have for teachers in Catholic schools?
2. What is your response to this quote?

Ford (1986) discusses the professional responsibilities and the private lives of teachers in Catholic schools. He states 'Undoubtedly the known behaviour of a teacher both in and out of school could affect the moral outlook of his/her pupils for the better or the worse'. This is why the new RE teacher should understand the professional and personal dimensions of teaching. The area of the private life of the teacher is one for the individuals involved. The school has no right to enquire about these matters provided they remain out of the public domain. More to the point, students have no right to ask about these matters. Teachers who allow themselves to be quizzed by students about how they choose to live their lives are not respecting the boundaries of proper professional teacher conduct. Recognise that if you choose to work in a Catholic school then you are agreeing to work within the parameters of a certain tradition and ethos. You are of course under no obligation to work in the Catholic school system.

As part of their professional lives teachers must respect the integrity of the school and its relationship with the Church. Catholic schools are integral parts of the mission and function of the Church. People who work in schools are expected not to contradict what the Church teaches, since this forms a vital part of the ethos of the school. This is especially important for RE teachers in the classroom. Mutual respect is called for. It also speaks to the professionalism of the teacher. If the RE teacher does not agree with a particular aspect of Church teaching this remains his or her own opinion, but this should not become a forum for disagreement, which can disrupt the culture and atmosphere of the school. In other words, the classroom is not the place for the RE teacher to air his or her disagreements with the Church.

The Catholic School on the Threshold of the Third Millennium

> In the Catholic school, 'prime responsibility for creating this unique Christian school climate rests with the teachers, as individuals and as a community'. Teaching has an extraordinary moral depth and is one of man's most excellent and creative activities, for the teacher does not write on inanimate material, but on the very spirits of human beings. The personal relations between the teacher and the students, therefore, assume an enormous importance and are not limited simply to giving and taking. Moreover, we must remember that teachers and educators fulfill a specific Christian vocation and share an equally specific participation in the mission of the Church, to the extent that 'it depends chiefly on them whether the Catholic school achieves its purpose'.
>
> CSTTM 19

QUESTIONS

1. What do you think is the extraordinary moral depth of teaching?

2. How is the contribution of teachers to Catholic schools described?

3. How are students described above?

ACTIVITY 17.1

> At the start of this chapter you were asked, 'Do you have any anxieties about teaching religious education?' How would you respond now?

The Sacred Congregation for Catholic Education. (1982). *Lay Catholics in schools: Witnesses to faith*. Homebush, NSW: St Paul Publications.

Congregation for Catholic Education. (1997). *The Catholic school on the threshold of the Third Millennium*. Homebush, NSW: St Paul Publications.

Ford, N. (1986). *Professional responsibility and the private lives of teachers in Catholic schools*. Homebush: St Paul Publications.

Rymarz, R. (2012a). Faithful dissent? Tackling the immediate issues facing religious educators in Canadian Catholic Schools – A response to McDonough. *International Studies in Catholic Education, 4* (1), 82-91.

Rymarz, R. (2012). Isn't there a town named after him? Content knowledge and teacher training in religious education. *Journal of Religious Education, 60* (2), 37-46.

CHAPTER 18

The Religious Education Teacher

> According to *The Catholic School* published in 1977 by the Sacred Congregation for Catholic Education, the success of the Catholic "depends not so much on the subject matter or methodology as on the people who work there".
>
> CS 43
>
> - Do you agree with this statement?
> - What implications does this have for teachers who work in Catholic schools and for RE teachers in particular?

> "We awake today, not to a secular Canada but to a polarized Canada. A solid core of people continue to value faith; but a significant core do not. A significant proportion remain in the middle – something like the politically undecided – dropping in and not dropping out".
>
> Bibby, R. (2012). *A new day: The resilience and restructuring of religion in Canada*, 10. Ebook available from http://www.reginaldbibby.com/images/A_NEW_DAY_Sept_12_2012.pdf
>
> - Do you agree with this statement?
> - What implications does this have for teachers who work in Catholic schools and for RE teachers in particular?

Three Teachers

Vignette 1. Kathy – a seasoned RE teacher

Kathy is married and her children are now adults. She started teaching in Catholic schools in 1971. In her career she has been a classroom teacher, Religious Education Coordinator and a Deputy Principal. She has also had some time away from schools when her children were young. Over the years Kathy has had a long involvement in her parish. Kathy has experienced many changes in her time in Catholic education.

Kathy and many others like her will soon retire from teaching in Catholic schools. When they go they will leave will cherished memories of teaching RE "at the coalface" that is the practical wisdom of being a good RE teacher. Here are some of Kathy recollections on her career as a RE teacher:

> I started teaching before I got married. It was hard in those days because we were not well paid and we had huge classes. We still occasionally used the catechism but we were aware of new approaches centred on the Good

News Bible. I then had a long break from teaching after I married and started to have children. When I returned in the 1970s things had changed even further. The nuns were leaving the school I worked in and I still remember the parents' reaction, largely negative, when it was announced that the school would soon be appointing its first lay principal. In RE we placed great emphasis on the experience of students but teaching RE day in and day out was hard work. There were also big changes in Catholic life in this period that I think were very significant for schools. When I was growing up we didn't question ourselves or the Church much. Most of the teachers in schools were also involved in parish life but in more recent times this connection has been broken. I've seen it in my own children; they are not religious in the same way as people of my generation.

- Try and imagine yourself in Kathy's situation. What do you think are some of the major issues for Kathy as a RE teacher?
- How does the Catholic school system replace teachers like Kathy?

Vignette 2. Damian – growing up in the 1980s

Damian was born in 1979. His experience of teaching in schools dates from the 1990s. Growing up Catholic in the 1980s was very different from earlier times. There was a great deal more freedom to do and say what you thought. At the same time there was a lot less support and guidance from mentors and other authority figures. There was much less emphasis, however, on the difference between Catholics and other groups in society. Damian's connection with the Church is much more precarious than previous generations. He was never a member of Catholic organisations at parish or young adult level. He can't remember ever having fasted or doing things because *that's what Catholics did*. He eventually qualified as a teacher. Here are some of Damian's reflections on teaching religious education:

> I sort of drifted into teaching and RE was never my strong point. I was much happier teaching literacy and numeracy. In the beginning it was tough because I lacked background and the students were unmotivated (perhaps the two were connected!). On a personal level my own life began to change about this time. I got married and last year we had our first child. This made me start to question what I valued in life and where I was heading. I am a Catholic but many of my family and most of my friends have drifted away from the Church. As I work in Catholic education I always maintained a connection with Church and began to rexamine where I stood on things. I started to get into RE teaching a bit more and saw it as something that could help students think more clearly about some of the big issues in life. I've recently enrolled in a course that will help develop my skills as a RE teacher. I think I might make a real go of being an RE teacher – who knows I may even on day be a deputy principal specializing in RE.

- Do you think Damian's approach to RE would differ from Kathy's?

- If so, in what way?
- Try and imagine a conversation between Kathy and Damian about how or what to teach in religious education time.
- Which one would relate better to students?

Vignette 3. Claudia – a RE teacher for the now

Claudia has just started her teaching career. This is also her first professional, full-time job. She has done RE as part of her teacher training but does not feel well qualified to teach the subject. She lives at home with her parents and plans to do so for some time. She is happy to call herself Catholic but has never really been that into religion. Some of her school friends went to World Youth Day, she thought about it but in the end gave it a miss. Claudia is a good example of the "options" generation. She has lots of paths open to her about how she lives her life. To her and many of her peers obligation has been replaced by choice. Here are some of Claudia's thoughts on teaching religious education:

> I'm really nervous about teaching in general but RE in particular. I'm just scared that I don't know enough. At Uni we were told that RE has the same demands as other subjects but in other areas we seem to have clearer instructions about what to do. I am also aware that students today do not seem all that interested in religion, but then again neither was I when I was at school. The fact that the Church is always in the news for all the wrong reasons also doesn't increase my confidence. On my teaching rounds I went to one school where RE didn't have much status and the teachers there found it a lot of work. At other schools, however, everyone was more positive and the teachers were great. They helped me a lot with lesson planing and finding resources. I just want to be a successful teacher.

- What advice would you give Claudia as she starts her RE teaching career?
- How do you think the life experiences of Kathy, Damian and Claudia will influence the way they approach RE teaching?
- Which teacher do you most relate to?

We are letting them [students] down, sending many, and probably most, of them out into the world without the basic intellectual tools and most basic formation needed to think and express even the most elementary of reasonably defensible moral thoughts and claims. And that itself, we think, is morally wrong (p.61).

- Do you agree with this statement?
- What implications does it have for RE teachers today?

Smith, C., Christoffersen, K., Davidson, H. and Snell Herzog, P. (2011). *Lost in transition: The dark side of emerging adulthood.* New York: Oxford University Press, 2011

Some Perspectives on the RE teacher

There are many ways to initiate a discussion about the role of RE teachers in contemporary schools. There is an established literature on this topic and below are two extracts from Church documents in the subject:

> In the Catholic school, "prime responsibility for creating this unique Christian school climate rests with the teachers, as individuals and as a community". Teaching has an extraordinary moral depth and is one of man's most excellent and creative activities, for the teacher does not write on inanimate material, but on the very spirits of human beings. The personal relations between the teacher and the students, therefore, assume an enormous importance and are not limited simply to giving and taking. Moreover, we must remember that teachers and educators fulfil a specific Christian vocation and share an equally specific participation in the mission of the Church, to the extent that "it depends chiefly on them whether the Catholic school achieves its purpose".
>
> The Catholic School on the Threshold of the Third Millennium (25)

ACTIVITY 18.1

According to The Catholic School on the Threshold of the Third Millennium:

- Who do teachers have prime responsibility for?
- What has enormous implications?
- What is described as a specific Christian vocation?

The religion teacher is the key, the vital component, if the educational goals of the school are to be achieved. But the effectiveness of religious instruction is closely tied to the personal witness given by the teacher; this witness is what brings the content of the lessons to life. Teachers of religion, therefore, must be men and women endowed with many gifts, both natural and supernatural, who are also capable of giving witness to these gifts; they must have a thorough cultural, professional, and pedagogical training, and they must be capable of genuine dialogue.

> Most of all, students should be able to recognise authentic human qualities in their teachers. They are teachers of the faith; however, like Christ, they must also be teachers of what it means to be human. This includes culture, but it also includes such things as affection, tact, understanding, serenity of spirit, a balanced judgment, patience in listening to others and prudence in the way they respond, and, finally, availability for personal meetings and conversations with the students. A teacher who has a clear vision of the Christian milieu and lives in accord with it will be able to help young people develop a similar vision, and will give them the inspiration they need to put it into practice.
>
> The Religious Dimension of Education in a Catholic School (96)

ACTIVITY 18.2

According to The Religious Dimension of Education in a Catholic School:

- How is the religion teacher described?
- What do you understand by the phrase teachers of what it means to be human?
- What is a clear vision of the Christian milieu?

ACTIVITY 18.3

After reading the two extracts above, try answering the following questions or discussing them with others:

- What is your reaction to the two extracts above?
- What do they tell us about the role of the teacher and RE teacher in a Catholic school?
- Do you agree with these views?
- Try to make a list of what is expected of teachers and religion teachers from the extracts above.

The Skills of the RE teacher

> ### *The RE teacher as hero*
>
> When thinking about the skills and abilities of the RE teacher it is important to have realistic expectations. If this is done then what is sometimes called the *hero model* is avoided. The hero model makes the RE teacher into a person who displays a complete range of complex, highly developed skills and attributes. The danger in thinking about RE teachers as heroes is that it can be quite discouraging, especially for new RE teachers. The intention here is not to describe a hero teacher. Rather it is to look analytically at the range of skills and abilities that can be attributed to a good RE teacher. What is important is that RE teachers be able to think about their roles as involving a range of skills needed rather than excelling in each dimension all the time – only heroes are able to so this!

One way to consider the skills of the RE teacher is to think about them as categories. This does not mean that the various categories do not overlap or that the qualities mentioned only apply to RE teachers. The skills of a good teacher tend to transcend subject boundaries and are difficult to distinguish completely. Naming different categories does, nonetheless, provide a conceptual framework in which the role of the RE teacher can be discussed.

1. RE Teacher as Teaching Professional

> "As a principal what I am looking for in a teacher who is new to my staff is one who can work within the professional constraints of the job. By that I mean they work as part of the team, they get to class on time, they do their marking and they make an effort to keep up with new developments…"

The issues raised by the principal in the quote above all refer to professional aspects of the role of the RE teacher. This includes being able to work well with other teachers. This is an important aspect of a teacher's life, especially in primary schools. Most schools work within a collaborative framework. The professional demands of RE teaching include aspects such as appropriate planning of lessons and Units of Work. Establishing links with other teachers via professional networks is also an important aspect of the professional responsibilities of RE teachers. At a school level, the professional RE teacher is well aware of the school culture and the various policies and frameworks that have been established at the school. In general they know what is expected of them and can meet these demands.

2. Content Knowledge and the RE teacher

Some time ago, one of the authors was working with a group of educators on developing RE Units of Work. As an illustration, some instances from the life of Mary were given. The subsequent explanation did not go well and the presenter realised that the group was not following what was being said. On questioning the group it emerged that many of the teachers had only the most basic understanding of Mary and her importance to Catholic culture and theology. With this sort of background it is impossible to teach about Mary with a high level of educational sophistication.

Good RE teachers need to have a competent level of content knowledge. This is especially important if the teacher is working within an educational understanding of the discipline. Like any subject, if the RE teacher is only " a page ahead" of her students she will struggle to be credible. Remember that students have an almost forensic ability to detect insincerity of the part of the teacher. Content knowledge here relates to the teacher's understanding of the various disciplines that underpin RE. These are subject areas such as theology, scripture studies and philosophy. How much the teacher should know is a difficult question to answer. On one hand teachers are not expected to have extensive post graduate qualifications. This is impractical, as well as being of dubious educational value. On the other hand, teachers must have enough expertise to feel confident in the discipline and be able to use their knowledge to fashion the teaching and learning strategies they use in the classroom.

The value of content knowledge is seen in the ability of the RE teacher to extend a topic as well as developing a theme sequentially.

ACTIVITY 18.4

> Imagine that you were asked to teach a unit on the Eucharist. Think of a particular year level and ask:

- What is the most sophisticated content that you could teach at this level?
- How would you teach this unit differently at different levels of the school?
- What content would be covered?

The depth of a teacher's content knowledge is crucial to how a theme or unit is developed. For example, in dealing with a topic such as Mary, this can be introduced as a simple narrative outlining her life as highlighted in the gospels. To proceed further requires a more sophisticated understanding. After presenting the story of Mary's life other themes, such as Mary's response to God's call, could be presented. Beyond this a teacher with good content knowledge could explore some of the implications of our thinking about Mary on how we understand Jesus. Without adequate content knowledge a teacher is likely to remain at the level of teaching students the narrative of Mary's life. Good content knowledge opens up many more educational possibilities.

3. *The Importance of Good Teaching*

Students and others often remark about the teaching skills of particular individuals with terms such as: she is a born teacher, when he teaches I really understand, or she is a great teacher. What is being recognised in these and other comments is that teaching skills are something that set apart the good teacher from a teacher who may have good content knowledge but is unable to share this knowledge with others. The discussion of what constitutes the exact nature of good teaching would take far more space than is available in this book. Nonetheless, it is important to recognise the centrality of what some authors call ***pedagogical content knowledge***. This involves being able to communicate to learners of a variety of ages, abilities and backgrounds difficult and new concepts. As well as being able to reformulate key ideas, the good RE teacher recognises the importance of a range of strategies, such as being able to use one's voice well, to repeat important pieces of information a number of times and to be alert and sensitive to responses from the class.

ACTIVITY 18.5

> Think back to teachers that you had when you were at school. What distinguished the good ones? Try to be as specific as possible. To assist you in this task try completing sentences such as Mrs Thompson was a good teacher because she… or Mr Bielak was great because he always…

4. *The Human Dimension of RE Teaching*

Some of the strongest memories that students have of their teachers are of their human qualities. They recall that certain teachers were kind, sensitive, considerate and joyous. At the same time they recall, perhaps with greater vigour, those who did not display these qualities. Often what was actually taught had less lasting impact or is more difficult to recall. This is a salutary message for all teachers, not just those in RE. It is very important to treat students with dignity and respect.

> *Some time ago one of the authors observed a teacher instructing a group of primary school students about the Eucharist. The rhetoric of the lesson was impressive. The Eucharist is God's great gift of love to us, in the Eucharist we meet God in a special way, the Eucharist is a great celebration – the list could go on and on. The teacher knew all the right answers. At one point in the lesson the students were asked to line up for practice for their First Communion. Here the language turned. The teacher scolded the students very harshly, using anger and sarcasm, for minor transgressions such as standing in the wrong place or not having at the ready the prepared prayer sheet. What the students were learning about at one level was the Eucharist as the great banquet of God. At another level they were hearing that the Eucharist was the type of thing where you'd better make sure you stand in the right spot and know your prayers otherwise someone in authority will scream at you and humiliate you in front of your friends and parents. Which message do you think will endure?*

The point of the story above is to express the simple idea that teachers need to be individuals who display strong human qualities. Professionalism, good content knowledge and teaching skills will not overcome a lack of virtue. This does not mean that RE teachers have to be one step away from canonisation to be effective. This is, again, the hero model of RE teaching. It does mean, however, that good RE teachers see the human dimension in what they are doing. They value the interaction with other people – in this case predominantly young people. Good RE teachers are not bitter, angry, resentful, mocking or sarcastic. They can empathise with students and enjoy working with them.

Good RE teachers know their students

When interviewing good RE teachers a number of years ago, one feature stood out. The teachers had an extensive and individualised knowledge of the students in their classes. They were able to identify, amongst other things, students who were:

- academically strong and those who had learning difficulties
- likely to speak out in discussions
- improving and those who were a worry – that is, something was affecting their usual performance
- *combustible* – that is, should never be seated together
- genuinely striving to find meaning in their lives

This makes the point that good RE teachers have almost a natural interest in their students and are able to individualise them. They do not see them as an undistinguished mass.

ACTIVITY 18.6

> List some of the human qualities that you think are important for RE teachers to display. Which do you think is the most important?

Another aspect of the human dimension of RE teaching is the ability to recognise your own talents and limitations. To take an extreme example there are some individuals who do not have the personal qualities that are needed to make a good RE teacher. These are not only people who display some of the negative characteristics listed earlier. It could include individuals who are very shy and do not like talking in public or drawing attention to themselves. On a positive note good RE teachers are aware of their strengths and try to utilise these to the best of their ability. A teacher who has musical gifts, for example, should be prepared to share these with students. Similarly, teachers with exuberant and invigorating personalities should not be afraid to let these attributes permeate their teaching.

5. RE Teacher as Witness

> Modern man listens more willingly to witnesses than to teachers, and if he does listen to teachers, it is because they are witnesses.
>
> EV 41

The quote above is from Pope Paul VI's Evangelii *Nuntiandi*.

ACTIVITY 18.6

> What implications, if any, does this quote have for RE teachers? Do you think it is accurate? Can you recall any teachers from your past who were witnesses to what they taught? If so how would you describe them?

In the past thirty years schools in general, and schools associated with religious traditions in particular, have experienced profound change. One aspect of this change has been the increasing pluralistic nature of Church affiliated schools. One way this is demonstrated is in the variety of faith commitments of teachers, students and parents who make up school communities. In the past it was an easy association to make that most people associated with the school would have a strong connection with the faith tradition of the school. In Catholic schools, for example, this was often expressed in terms of most students and staff going to Mass on Sunday. Today those students and teachers who strongly identify with the faith tradition may be less numerous. This changed reality brings with it challenges for the school's identity and its role as an educative part of the wider Christian community. The school should be a place where students have an experience of the Gospel being lived out and where Christian witness is modelled. In terms of the ethos of Catholic schools there is an expectation that the school be a place where students are invited to share in a faith response. RE teachers play an important role in animating the ethos of the school. Part of this role is to witness to the values that the school represents.

A REC commented that students in schools have a *forensic ability* to detect hypocrisy on the part of teachers. If a teacher says something and then does the opposite the credibility of the teacher is in question. These issues have great relevance for RE teachers because they relate to the important theme of the witness of the RE teacher. Witness can be understood at a number of levels. It can be seen as the attitude that the teacher brings to the class. Teachers must witness to the importance of RE by bringing with them a positive and committed attitude. This is also part of the professional responsibilities of the RE teacher. Students do not generally respond well to those who do not appear to regard what they are doing as a serious and important activity. On another level witness refers to the way the teacher embraces the values and ethos of the school. At the heart of this ethos in Catholic schools is some statement about the importance of the Christian culture that the school springs from. At a deeper level still is the witness RE teachers give to the importance of their own spiritual journey. RE teachers should feel comfortable with their own faith commitment and be able to identify with the life and worship of the Tradition. RE teachers who live out a sincere conviction to model their lives on the person of Christ are valued by schools because they make the essential link between the ideals of the school and the invaluable dimension of praxis, that is, a lived out reality. This type of modelling can be very important for students today.

It is important to distinguish between genuine witness and sentimental piety. Witness involves a robust commitment on the part of the RE teacher to a life-long journey that now involves helping others on their journey of faith. Doubt, uncertainty and lapses are only to be expected. This only makes the witness of the teacher more authentic because it resonates with the journeys of other believers over the centuries.

Congregation for Catholic Education. (1997). *The Catholic school on the threshold of the third millennium.* Homebush: St Paul Publications.

Pope Paul VI. (1976). *Evangelii Nuntiandi.* Homebush: St Paul Publications.

Shulman, L. (1994). Knowledge and teaching: Foundations of the new reform. *Harvard Educational Review* 57(1).

Sikes, P and Everington, J. (2001). Becoming an RE teacher: a life history approach. *British Journal of Religious Education, 24* (1), 8-20.

The Congregation for Catholic Education. (1988). *The religious dimension of education in a Catholic school.* Homebush: St Paul Publications.